Erratı

The Forgotten Army

Please note the following corections.
Page 3. Last paragraph Line 10.
For Clem Attlee, read Neville Chamberlain

Page 92. First paragraph first line.
For March 1994, read March 1944.

Page 103. First paragraph third line.
For Land Rover, read
Jeep, or Land Rover type of Military vehicle.

Page 109. Len Sheppard credit
Should read **COFEPOW.**
Not FEPOW.

Erratum

The Forgotten Army

Please note the following corrections
Page 3. Last paragraph Line 10.
For Clem Attlee, read Neville Chamberlain

Page 92. First paragraph first line
For March 1994, read March 1944

Page 103. First paragraph third line
For Land Rover, read
Jeep, or Land Rover type of Military vehicle.

Page 109. Len Sheppard credit
Should read **COFEPOW.**
Not FEPOW.

The Forgotten Army

by

Roy Yates

Published by Infinity Junction, Neston, Cheshire

ISBN 1-904101-00-3

First published in 2001 by
INFINITY JUNCTION
PO Box 64
Neston DO
CH64 0WB
UK

Cover picture selected from a collection of royalty free Coral Corporation stock photos from VNU Publications. Other photographs copyright of the author, or courtesy of the Far East Prisoners of War Social Club and The Daily Mail newspaper

Layout and typesetting by InfinityJunction.com
Printed and bound in Great Britain by
Warwick Printing Company Limited
Warwick
CV34 4DR
England

*To my dear brother
Leonard.
In acknowledgement of
his computer skills in
writing this narrative*

The author, sometime after release

Chapter I

My Call To Arms

I was born in the year 1920 and of course in 1939 I would be 19 years old, up to that time my life was much the same as any other. The year 1939 however, changed everything. It was the beginning of the second world war. I was in the employ of the London Midland & Scottish Railway Co. Trentham Railway station at this time. About 100 yards from the station there was a branch line to Florence Colliery and Trentham Gardens, you could buy a railway ticket on Stoke station to take you straight into the gardens, the branch line was quite busy at weekends. This was a problem because if I was on the late shift I did not finish until 10:30pm. but had to be back on duty again Monday morning at 6:15am. So I usually stayed overnight. Living in Stafford it was 12 miles to Trentham this of course involved a one hour cycle ride, so I had to be on the road at 5:15am. It would be interesting to note that in those days even though you could buy a new car for £98 there were very few on the road. The average weekly wage would be about £2:50 to £3:00 and cigs were 20 for 11pence and one half penny.

During early summer of 1939 most people in this country were becoming more concerned that war was not far away. The government had introduced military service, anyone 20-21 not in a essential occupation was being called up to do a period of military training, (they were called The Militia).

On the continent at the Eastern Front Adolf Hitler's troops had met with little or no resistance. Czechoslovakia had fallen to his invading army and they were now already approaching Poland when he was advised to halt or else Britain would be forced to take up arms. Needless to say he ignored this country's threats. His advancing troops entered Poland on the 1st September 1939. Great Britain honoured its pledge when Neville Chamberlain, Conservative Prime Minister broadcast on radio at 11:15am on Sunday 3rd September 1939 "That this country is now at war with Germany." France, Canada, Australia and New Zealand declared War the same day. Strangely we had an air raid warning that same day but it was a false alarm. In the evening our King George VI broadcast a rallying message to the Empire. A few days later on the 6th September 1939 America declared that they were strictly neutral towards all Nations involved in the conflict.

Within days a British Expeditionary Force was despatched to France. The contestants confronted one another from behind their Siegfried (German) and Maginot (French) Lines. These were concrete fortress lines reminiscent of the 1914-1918 War. The fortresses consisted of underground tunnels with a concrete and barbed wire fence entanglement above ground. Needless to say as aircraft were increasingly involved as a preliminary source of attack these fortresses proved to be of no significant form of defence.

My thoughts during those first days of conflict were with the lads in France, I longed to be with them but until I was 20 year's old it would not be possible. People were also saying that it would be all over by Christmas. How wrong they were. I had to wait till the end of February 1940, when I received notification to report to a local Church Room for my medical, I passed A1. Subsequently I received my call up papers ordering me to report to Whittington Barracks Lichfield, on the morning of 18th April 1940. I remember it well. On the Wednesday evening 17th April I finished work at 10-30pm cycled home from Trentham and the next morning took the first available train to Lichfield, (not realising the terrible and traumatic times the following five and a half years would bring). I eventually arrived at Whittington Barracks, several other lads got off the same bus, we were directed to stand on the parade ground when a sergeant came marching across the square with a stick under his arm, he shouted, "stand up straight shoulders back, I'm going to be your mother for the next six weeks." He formed us into lines and bawled "follow me," we were led into a barrack room and told this would be our billet during our initial military training. The barrack room consisted of two rows of beds, one on each side of the billet, with a coal stove centrally situated for heating. This bed turned out to be one of the last one I had the pleasure of using until my release from captivity. Very soon after others had arrived we were marched to the QM Stores and issued with our kit consisting, kit bag, two suits of battle dress, one suit of denim for fatigues, one great coat, two pair of boots, two pair of grey socks, one side hat, one steel helmet, harness for back pack and haversack, two blankets and a ground sheet. Arriving back at the barrack room with our kit we were told to remove all civvies and dress in denim. The strange thing about the kit, it was a good fit, when issued the Quarter Master looked at you and decided what size you were. Our civvies were forwarded and returned home, as we were not allowed to wear them for the duration of the war. Very soon after our call up we had to take turns keeping the barrack room clean usually one day's duty, my turn eventually arrived. In the late afternoon I sat by the stove having a warm. The sergeant came in and saw a piece of coal on the plinth he said "What's this," then picked each of the buckets which were full of coal and emptied them across the barrack room floor. He roared: "Now get that bloody lot up and polish up afterwards," it took me till bedtime and I could not go out that night.

During the first six weeks we were trained to use all small arms, bayonet practice, field craft, marching, physical training, route marching, square drill and everything else which makes a British soldier one of the finest and fittest combatants on earth.

Early June 1940 saw our platoon pass out and we were suddenly posted to Sheffield. Vehicles met us at the railway station and to our surprise we were dropped off at private houses and had a bedroom to ourselves and we lived with local families for several days.

News was filtering through about the Nazi purge of all Jews in Germany and elsewhere, concentration camps were rapidly filling and the occupants ultimately being put to death by starvation and the gas chamber. The war at sea was becoming quite vicious several battleships of ours and Germany had been sunk. There was also a noticeable increase in activity in the air. The Battle of Britain had begun. Activity on the Western Front was bad news, the German army had made a dramatic push along the 120 mile border of Holland and Belgium. The retreating allies could not hold them. Holland had fallen on the 13th of May. A few days earlier on the 11th of May due to the serious situation Clem Attlee had resigned and Winston Churchill the then First Sea Lord, took over as Prime Minister. The retreating B.E.F. (British Expeditionary Force) gallantly fought from house to house and were ultimately driven on to the beaches at Dunkirk, we all now know of the valiant efforts of the RAF, Navy, Merchant Navy, and 100's of other small boats which took part in the evacuation of Dunkirk, finally ending on the 5th of June 1940. Many historians believe that had Hitler followed up with an all out attack on this Island we could have lost the war. Winston Churchill expected it when he made that gripping speech. "Even though large tracts of Europe are in the grip of Nazi rule, we shall go on to the end, we shall fight on the seas and oceans, we shall fight in the air, we shall defend our Island whatever the cost. we shall fight on the beaches, we shall fight on the landing grounds, in the fields, in the streets, in the hills, we shall never surrender. Even if, which I do not for one moment believe this Island or part of it is subjugated and starving, then our Empire armed and guarded by the British Fleet will carry on the struggle, until in Gods good time the New World with all its power and might set forth to the liberation and rescue of the old."

The reason we had been posted to Sheffield soon became obvious, the depleted B.E.F. on arrival back in the UK was sent to various parts of the country to re equip and re group. In the process I found myself in the First Sixth South Staffordshire Regiment of the 59th division of the British Army. Which eventually, I have since been led to believe, became the first invasion troops.

The following months were spent practising warfare on the Yorkshire Moors, directing people into air raid shelters during air raids which by then happened daily. I was finally selected for specialised training and was sent to Catterick to be trained as a wireless operator by the Royal Corps Of Signals at their training camp. During these months it will be remembered that many towns were very heavily bombed, particularly London and Coventry, children were evacuated out of the cities and billeted with other families in country districts. The Italian dictator Mussolini joined Hitler and declared war on the Allies June 11th 1940, by the 24th June the whole of Northern France came under Nazi rule. General De Gaulle and many other French servicemen escaped to Gt. Britain. It should be realised that at this time we alone were in conflict with the might of Germany and Italy. What a fight it turned out to be. Throughout the coming weeks 'The Battle of Britain' really got underway. Our Spitfire and Hurricane fighters chased and fought the might of the German bombers and fighters day and night, with dog fights over Britain and the channel. It was thrilling to see the action if you happened to be on watch during the bombing raids. By the 13th of July, Germany had lost 108 bombers and fighters, 72 had been brought down in one week. We, of course also lost many airmen, so severe was the Nazi onslaught.

The process of re equipping and re grouping the army continued. The Divisional H.Q of the 59th eventually settled at Barnard Castle, Co. Durham. I rejoined the division after six weeks of training with various radios used by the Corps of signals. I became efficient using Morse code, theodolites, and all aspects of communication even including driving lessons. As the result of my training I was eventually posted to a new Corps called 59th Recce Corps. We were supplied with tracked armoured vehicles and tyre armoured vehicles, we called them AFV's. (Armoured Fighting Vehicles) So my job was to operate the radio as a communication link between company commanders of the infantry battalion to which I was attached. Our function was to go ahead of the infantry to test the fire power of the enemy and also engage small pockets of resistance. As this was a dangerous job we were given extra pay. However, there was no enemy to fight in this country, so our time was spent in mock battles on the North Yorkshire Moors. But the serious work became defending this country. So most of the time was spent in buildings along the North East Coast with my radio and the infantry in dugouts on the beach front, of course during the battle of Britain no civilians were allowed on the sea front. I spent time at Redcar, Saltburn on Sea and several other small coastal villages. Whilst at Redcar a radio message came through to stand too, I had a warning that the Germans were attempting to make a landing on the South East Coast. The attack however, did not take place, probably due to bad weather conditions. At this time the Germans were bombing us ceaselessly, and from my position I could watch them coming in from the sea, amidst puffs of white from our ack ack, (Anti Aircraft Battery) occasionally a plane would be hit and drop into the sea, I never saw anyone go out to look for survivors so if they did not make it to the shore they drowned.

Most of the cities and big towns in the UK. were now receiving the full might of the German bombers, London and Coventry receiving the worst attacks, Coventry Cathedral was demolished, even Buckingham Palace was bombed. We took our fair share in the North East because of the steel works in the area. We eventually moved to Consett, Co Durham, the home of the steelworks. During our stay in the town we were invited to visit the works and see the whole process, nothing of particular interest was being made except that when the lengths of steel were being rolled out from the press it emitted very loud bangs.

In the services one always tends to make someone a close friend. My friend was called Douglas. His home town happened to be about eighteen miles from mine. He told me that he had a girl and that they were engaged to be married. One day we sat talking when the mail arrived, as we sat reading his manner seemed to change, I enquired what was the matter, he said the letter was from his girl breaking the engagement. It was a terrible shock to him, particularly being in the services and away from home. In the days that followed he didn't seem to get over it. One evening we were getting ready to go out, he suddenly said to me, "If volunteers are requested to go abroad I am going to volunteer, there is nothing left for me in this life".

We were now into early September 1941, strangely, our officer came into our billet one day and called us all together. He informed us that he had received a request from the 18th Division for two signal operators to bring them up to full strength to go abroad, Doug. stood up saluted and said, "I'll go Sir" the room went quiet, no one else spoke. I felt rather uneasy wondering what to do. I couldn't let him go on his own. I felt very hot and uncomfortable, suddenly without another thought I stood up saluted and said "I'll go with him Sir". (This decision proved to be the most crucial of my whole life. The realisation of this did not become apparent until many years later when, being a keen amateur photographer, I decided to take some pictures of the flower borders in our local park, to get a higher view point I wandered up the steps of the War Memorial and my eyes were drawn to a plaque depicting the shaft head of a coal mine, which was of course the shoulder flash I had when in the 59th Division. The plaque was a memorial of the almost wiping out of the entire Division during the "D" Day landings in 1944. I then realised and believed that because of my care and consideration for a comrade, the Almighty God had guided me safely through the terrible years of captivity, which at the same time prevented me from going to France on "D" Day.)

Within days we were given railway tickets to go on embarkation leave. The night before we were due to catch the train from Newcastle upon Tyne we decided to get drunk, and to ensure we had not far to walk in a drunken state visited the pub across the road from the billet. I had three pints of beer and eight or was it eleven rums, can't remember. I walked back to the billet cursing, I still felt sober and went to bed, in the war there were no beds as such, we just spread out our ground sheet on the floor, folded a blanket to lie on and a blanket over the top of me, I used my kit bag as a pillow. I could not have been asleep long when I was awakened with a splitting head, my eyes seemed to be rolling, I was choking for breath and the ceiling appeared to be coming down on top of me, I longed to be sick and crawled to the door of the billet and eventually my stomach obliged. I must have lain there sometime because I realised I was quite cold, and crawled back to my space on the floor. I still could not get my breath and wished I was dead I felt that ill. There was no sleep for me that night, I still felt ill at 7 am I was packing all my kit together as a Landrover drove up to the billet to take us both to the station. We caught the 8.45 a.m train from Newcastle and decided to go to the dining car for some breakfast. We staggered along the coaches and fell on the seat of the diner, the attendant came to the table, took one look at us and said, "would you like some coffee first sirs". After the coffee and a good breakfast we felt a little better, but we were still staggering when we changed trains at Tamworth Staffs.

During the period of leave, with both families living close, I was able to meet Doug's parents and his sister. The period of leave went all too quickly and strangely we had a bit of luck. Our orders were to report to HQ Company, 5th Battalion The Loyal Regiment, 18th Div. Recce Corps, stationed at Madeley Staffs, which was only a few miles from our homes. (Whilst researching Land Forces records recently, I found that the 5th Loyals received an Honorary Distinction Badge for its services in Malaya.) The camp was situated in the village going through a small wood we entered a field with wooden buildings one of which would be our billet for the next three weeks. We joined up with the other lads in the signals section but we soon found out to our dismay that they were not very friendly, they were very cliquey and treated us as outcasts, any undesirable duties always came our way. Over the years since returning to civilian life their treatment towards me has been the subject of many nightmares. Therefore, the plaque I came across on the war memorial on that day in Stafford Park, brought back memories of many friends and mates in the 59th division with whom I had spent many months living and training. So much so I wanted to take steps to find out what happened to them. Their movements, and eventual involvement in the war.

The 59th Infantry Division was formed in August 1939 just before the United kingdom declared war on Germany. The Division was made up mostly of North and South Staffordshire Regiments with units of other Regiments from various parts of the Country, namely The Royal Norfolk Regiment, The East Lancashire Regiment, and the Royal Warwickshire Regiment. The Division was broken down into three brigades, The 176th, The 177th, and The 197th. Each Brigade was made up of three Battalions, each again split into four Companies of infantry. At that time the various units were spread out in various Counties of the UK. But it was interesting to note that Divisional HQ in September 1939 spent a short period of time in Burton Manor, Stafford. The Division was also supported by units of The Royal Corps of Signals, The Royal Artillery, Royal Engineers, Royal Army Service Corps, The Army Medical Corps, and The Reconnaissance Corps, (to which I belonged). In those early days units of the Division spent quite a lot of time training on Cannock Chase. Eventually the Division moved to the north east and this was where I joined up with them in the 1st 6th South Staffordshire Regiment on their return after their evacuation from Dunkirk.

The Division moved from the north east coast area soon after Douglas and I left them. In November 1941 the Division left England and moved to Northern Ireland and remained there until February 1943. I understand that their spell in that province was very enjoyable, although there was isolated incidents with the IRA. In February 1943 the Division returned to England and moved south and concentrated itself in and around Kent. They found themselves among many hundreds of thousands of men in other units from America. Canada and elsewhere. A complete Allied Army all waiting to hear the instruction to go over the water and invade France and push those damned arrogant Gerries back to where they came from.

They had to wait over another year, in which time their strength was built up both physically and supportively.

Under strict security the whole army moved into tent accommodation on and near the south coast. Suddenly, without warning operation, " Overlord" began. On the evening of the 5th of June 1944 advance airborne troops went in to secure vital positions needed to enable the seabourne invasion troops a foothold when going ashore. The 59th were in place to move out on the 17th, but bad weather set in and they had to wait until the25th of June which was the date they set off for the beaches of Normandy. They landed on the 26th without a single casualty and concentrated between Bayeux and Cruelly. They spent the next few days consolidating and preparing for their first confrontation with the German Army. It should be mentioned that on arrival in France all allied troops came under the overall command of Field Marshall Montgomery, that superb Commander everyone should have heard about. A man whose leadership was second to none

Ever since 'D Day' the British had been hammering on the German hinge at Caen, but despite continual strong pressure they were still holding firm and something had to be done to break their resistance. Field Marshall Montgomery gave orders for the 59th division to move into position and attack the strong enemy positions south of Caen. The area under attack was first to be softened up by heavy bombing and artillery bombardment. However, it soon became apparent that some of the German defences remained untouched, and in consequence the division suffered considerably with losses of dead and wounded. Unknown to the attacking forces the enemy had built a very useful trench system reminiscent of those used in world war one and some very well protected light and heavy machine gun positions manned by Panzer troops with a fanatical spirit of resistance.

My interest in what happened to the division led me to visit Whittington Barracks Lichfield, where I first tasted my introduction to military service. I was disappointed to hear that my barrack room had since been demolished. There was an air of utter quietness about the place. The main entrance is now protected with large metal doors firmly closed and locked. The surrounding wall protected with barbed wire. Its in full use by troops but I supposed IRA activity on the mainland has made troop protection more important.

A very interesting museum has been built on ground outside the barracks. I had to go in to have a look round and low and behold to my utter amazement, just inside the entrance I noticed a very large flag on which was displayed the pit head sign which was the 59th divisional identity flash which we stitched onto our battledress blouse. The exploits of the division were well and truly displayed together with all sorts of other memorabilia appertaining to both the 1st and 2nd world wars. My visit turned out to be very useful as I was introduced to a veteran who had served with the 7th Battalion South Staffordshire Regiment. His name is Richard Rutter. He kindly invited me to his home and we had quite a discussion about our personal involvement in the war. We seemed to be on the same wave length to the extent that we became somewhat can I say emotional. There was a welling up of sensitive feeling and we had to take our handkerchiefs out of our pockets as a few tears began to flow. After another cup of tea I left together with some books he has very kindly lent me from which I am able to write this episode of my story. He also gave me permission to print the very moving incident we talked about of his involvement in the attack just south of Caen between Galamanche and Bijude

I propose to write it in the first person just as he told me.

"I was with several mates we stood under this embankment as the grenades were coming over we threw them back, one fell between one of my mates legs, I shouted to him to throw it back when it went off, he went up in the air and came down like a rag doll, I thought that's it he's dead. We continued to exchange fire and one by one my mates were hit. I continued to fire with my LMG (light machine gun, we call them Bren guns) I shot at anything that I saw moving, my eyes would not see anything stationery. Suddenly I realized I was on my own they had killed my mates. I was filled with rage and madness, I had to kill the lot of them. I stood up uncaring of any danger and ran in a zig zag pattern towards the bastards. Firing until my Magazine ran out. I held my bren by its barrel and dropped into their trench bludgeoning them with the butt of my bren gun, I felt pain and must have gone unconscious because I began to be aware of things but I could not see through my eyes, I thought was I dead! Then I heard some birds singing, but I could not see, I put my finger up to my eye to force it open, I felt blood, I had been wounded over my left temple and the blood had run down my face and congealed. A chink of light appeared I couldn't feel my hands they were burned and were like sausages. As my eyes began to take in things around me I saw this German in the hole. He told me I was his prisoner. I couldn't have given a monkeys if I was his prisoner or he mine. I went unconscious again and when I woke up I saw that he was asleep. I slowly crept over towards him on my knuckles and took away his machine gun and stick grenades and went back to my side of the trench, I was now in a position to kill him, and I had every intention of doing it. I kept my eyes on him and when he woke up he asked me for a cigarette in german, I thought you cheeky bastard.I had some Woodbines in my battledress breast pocket, but my hands were so swollen and burned there was no way I could get them out so I made him understand that he could come and get them himself. He crawled over towards me and I picked up his gun in case he had ideas; he didn't. he took one out of the packet, they had all dried out and the tobacco was falling out, he dragged himself back to his side of the trench tapped the paper tube to get the tobacco together and lit it. I sat watching him trying to decide when I was going to kill him and I most surely was when I noticed blood on him. It turned out that he had a chest wound large enough to put your fist in. I did not have to kill him he died some time later. Eventually someone in my company rescued me, although they had assumed that I had been killed. I was taken to an American Field Hospital Unit to be given treatment to my wound and hands".

It should be realized that when a bren gun is fired continuously the barrel gets extremely hot and this was the reason Richard's hands were so burned and swollen. He told me that after treatment he returned to his unit as his trigger finger was OK.

Talking to Richard in his home I found him to be a very modest down to earth man who did not want to put any great emphasis on his solitary effort to try and kill off the whole bloody German Army, but I did find out that he was awarded the MM. For his courage and bravery.

The 59th's confrontation with the German Army in the Caen area eventually proved to be fatal, they suffered far too many killed and wounded. Re-enforcement was sparse almost non existent. After a brief rest they continued their campaign for several more weeks, gradually forcing the enemy to retreat and at the same time taking some prisoners.

Quite suddenly and without no real warning, 59th Division had ceased to exist. Overnight, five years training, and five weeks fighting had been relegated to the past. The Division was to be disbanded, its residue broken up and distributed to other Divisions.

Field Marshall Montgomery had written and told the sad news that, because of the acute shortage of trained reserves, particularly in the infantry, it would be necessary to break up the 59th Division His decision could not be questioned and was accepted with heavy hearts. How was this going to be achieved without any lowering of morale. After all that they had suffered together, all future battles were going to have to fought with strangers.

In lighter vein there were one or two incidents worth mentioning like,- the boche prisoner who was taken because he said it was safer to advance and be captured than retire to a shell- ridden start line'; the surprised British Officer and equally shocked German who jumped simultaneously through opposite windows into the same room, eyed each other nervously and hurriedly jumped out again.

Chapter II

War in the 18th Division

Having joined with our new Division, we did not care too much because each night we were able to go into town or visit our homes. Very soon after our arrival AFV's (armoured fighting vehicles) began to arrive we noticed they were painted a sandy colour, we therefore assumed we were destined for the desert. We were also issued with tropical kit. Movement of troops during the war was always kept a very close secret. The document from the war office stating the destination could not be opened by the officer in charge until a certain point had been reached in the journey. Perhaps I should mention here that the Reconnaissance Corps, (Recce Corps) was really a new unit in the British Army, we were in fact eventually joined to the Royal Armoured Corps, which of course is the tank regiment. Unlike the tanks our vehicles were lighter and more manoeuvrable. Our strategy in conflict would in fact save many lives of the infantry behind us. In the event that fire power of the enemy proved to be too great, we would be able to call up reinforcements from supporting artillery and the airforce, whilst still holding our position. World War Two has seen considerable changes in the way war is waged. From the bow and arrows with soldiers on horseback with pikes, fighting in small confined groups to the deep trench warfare with artillery in support as in World War One, even then war seemed to be confined to fighting between two trenches. Now technology has enabled a country to go to war without even setting foot on its opponent's territory. Foot troops are only needed for moping up operations, and dealing with small pockets of resistance etc.

During the third week in Madeley distinct signs were noticed that we would soon be on the move, one day we were told to dress in our best battle dress ready for parade at 11 am. as the hour approached we were marched and paraded in lines across the field in complete battle order kit. At about 11.45 a.m several cars drove into the field followed by a Rolls Royce with the Royal Emblem on the bonnet. Who should step out but the King and Queen, who then walked along our ranks and finally spoke to us all wishing us a safe journey and every success in our future engagements. The following day our equipment was loaded onto vehicles and we marched to the train. No one knew where we were going. Eventually our train drew into Avonmouth railway station, and very soon we walked up

the gangway of a very large ship, I noticed that it was called the 'Aronsay.'
Our kit bags had already been hoisted on board and we were instructed to
collect it and take below to the deck we were allotted. We found the deck
to be an open space and wondered about sleeping arrangements, if we slept
on the floor and the sea was rough we would be rolling about all over the
place. The answer soon became obvious, we were given hammocks. That
first night was hilarious, we had to grab a rail attached to the ceiling of the
deck and swing up into the hammock, some of the lads cracked it some did-
n't and finished on the floor. We eventually found them to be very comfortable as the swing of the hammock counteracted the roll of the ship and
believe me that ship found some rough seas. I and several other lads managed to get hold of some pieces of wood about 2 ft long and 1 inch square
from the ship's crew, these were used to spread the ropes at the end we
placed our head which made sleeping more comfortable. It was very warm
below decks so we slept without our blanket. It was a strange sight at night
when every one was in their hammocks the movement of the ship caused
them to swing rhythmically, we could not feel the movement though.

Within the hour of our arrival onboard we felt a slight vibration and
decided to go up on deck. The ship had already cast off and we began to
move away from the dockside, there was no one there to wave us goodbye.
Troop movements must be kept secret in war. The ship moved steadily
down the Severn estuary towards the open sea there was quite a chill breeze
blowing from the north east, the month was September 1941. At this time
on the continent the German Army having no one to fight on the Western
Front had turned its attention to the Eastern Front and was attacking
Russia. They were using 100 Divisions on a 1,800 mile front and now well
into Russian territory. A meeting had also taken place between Churchill
and Roosevelt. The President had stated that whilst the USA still remained
very neutral they wished to provide all the help we needed, under the "
Lease Lend" agreement. 20 Boeing Flying Fortress Bombers had already
been sent and were now in action. As we left the estuary a single naval
destroyer joined us our only protection. Under the Lease Lend Agreement
with the USA, most of the aid had to be transported by sea. The German
High Command responded by sending a fleet of submarines to patrol the
North Atlantic. These subs. had been attacking the convoys and had sunk
quite a number of our ships bringing guns, vehicles and other equipment to
help our war effort. So you can imagine how we felt going out onto the
high seas. We were helpless without the Navy. Our ship left the estuary and

strangely turned north east following the coast line, then a northerly direction keeping the Welsh coast in sight, we continued to travel north and eventually saw land on both sides of the ship, we were eventually told that we had entered the Firth of Clyde, The ship finally came to a standstill and dropped anchor, we found out that we were very close to Gourock. During the next 24 hrs several other ships arrived together with several destroyers and a battleship, the convoy was now complete.

Very early the next morning we felt that the ship had started to move and later going on deck there was no sight of land and still travelling north towards Greenland, it was obvious the Navy were concerned and wished to thwart the U Boat menace. (U- boat was the name of the German Subs.) The convoy also steered a zig zag course for the same reason. But where were we going? Life onboard soon became very boring, we had some physical training in the mornings, read books, there was quite a lot of freedom. Most of us got seasickness in the first few days, there was quite a swell and the Atlantic can give you quite a rough journey. We were asked if we would like to man the signalling lamp, it is about 10 inches across with metal slats inside the glass front, these are attached to a lever at the side of the lamp, which opens and closes the slats and thus creates the Morse signals. All ship's radios were silenced at sea because of the U-boats, so these lamps were the means of communication between the ships in the convoy.

Chapter III

We Meet The U.S. Navy

We had been travelling west after passing south of Greenland, I think we were about 5 days out and I happened to be on duty early on a Sunday morning, it is so vivid in my memory. It was just getting light, I began to hear a droning noise coming from the West, very soon the sky was full of planes, I was told, don't worry they are American, they are going to take over the convoy, I said "But America is not in the war." The ships officer just smiled and said, "You have seen nothing and know nothing." Very soon in the morning light specs began to appear on the western horizon. Later lights started flashing between our naval boats and the American boats. I said, "Bloody hell the whole of the American Fleet are here." There was an Aircraft Carrier, two battleships and God knows how many destroyers. Just like the Yanks, everything has to be done in a big way. They were travelling like speedboats round our convoy and making such a fuss it seemed as though they were tempting the U- boats to come and have a go. Our naval boats soon left us to return home. After several more uneventful days at sea, we came in sight of land, it was Halifax, Nova Scotia. The whole convoy drew into the dockyard (except the USA navy) and dropped anchor, it was late afternoon. That same evening we were told to pack everything up as we were going ashore next morning.

The following morning after breakfast we picked up our kit and went ashore onto the dockside. We hung about for several hours and during that time sat around on sacks filled with what felt like peas. One of the lads took his bayonet out and stuck it in one of the bags, we were very pleased to see loads of peanuts spewing out, well of course we all filled our pockets and ate nuts for days. Later we moved further along the dockside to another boat without any camouflage, it was quite smaller than the 'Aronsay.' I am not quite sure now but I think it was called 'MountVernon,' something like a large river boat. Believe it or not it was American, we were going to be travelling on American ships and they were still not in the war. Within 24 hrs the Germans knew and on the radio declared that they were going to sink the lot of us. Strangely the warning did not seem to bother any of us. We were more than pleased to go onboard, as the conditions for sleeping were much better, this time we had bunk bed's one above the other, each had a rail to prevent us falling out in rough weather. Our first meal late afternoon was tea, going down further below decks to the mess we had another surprise, the tables were decked with food of all kinds with fruit, real butter and cake on display. We all had our fill and felt Christmas had come early, great. Meals onboard the American ships were totally different, food was issued by the cafeteria system we each had a tray with about six compartments in it and as we moved along a counter chose what and how much of each item we wanted. This luxury was, however, short lived. During the evening meal next day the IC Troops came into the mess, in the British Army it is customary for an Officer to occasionally drop in whilst troops are having a meal to ask if there are any complaints, needless to say no one ever dared to complain. He gave one look at what we had been tucking into strode across to the cooks and said take all this away, these men will be too fat to fight when they go into action. Next day we were back on meagre rations and marg. In the army you are given just enough, you get up from the table still feeling hungry. But I can say, there was no doubt, we were all extremely fitter as a result of the rationing. The ship's canteen became our favourite source of enjoyment, very cheap sweets, chocolate, cigarettes and cigars, all American, we were able to buy cigarettes and cigars very cheaply. I remember cigs were about 6 cents a packet of 20, so we bought them by the carton holding 10 packets of 20, cigars were bought by the box. Soon it was a common sight to walk around the open top deck to see men sitting around reading a book and smoking a cigar.

We were now sailing south but not too far from land which could be faintly seen on the horizon, another strange thing began to happen. Several of the American crew could be seen leaning over the side of the boat, they were being seasick, so we assumed that they had never been on the high seas before. After three days at sea the weather began to get warmer, again wondering where we would end up. If it was North Africa what were we doing sailing down the coast of America. Going down to the galley for meals was becoming extremely uncomfortable, we found it necessary to strip to shorts only, the heat and humidity was so intense. The sea also seemed to be changing colour and looking over the side of the boat the water was getting clearer. Two more days passed and we began to approach land. Soon the anchor was lowered and we were told it was Trinidad. Once the boat had stopped the heat became more intense onboard, the crew opened all the portholes and gangway doors to try and draw in the very slight breeze off the sea, there was not a ripple on the water, just a slight swell, the breakers rolling onto the shore were of the purest white. Looking over the side of the boat one could see to quite a depth with lots of fish swimming about round the boat. The view was astounding, our thoughts were, to realise that spending a holiday on one of the Islands in the Caribbean would be wonderful. The heat below was now so uncomfortable we had been given permission to sleep on the deck, but we still had to go down to the galley for meals, even though we disposed of the food quickly, we still left a pool of perspiration on the floor where we had been sitting. After 24 hours we heard the anchor being raised and said thank God, at least we shall get a little breeze by moving. Sleeping on deck continued to be allowed and soon space began to be at a premium, if you did not book a space with your blanket early you missed out for that night. The journey after leaving Trinidad was the most boring three weeks I have ever spent, not one speck of land was seen during that time. The only respite being little ceremonies for the troops and crew when crossing the Equator, not everyone could take part but we all got a certificate. Eventually the weather turned very cold and we had to put on some extra clothing. Within two days the sea had become very rough, it was frightening on deck, one minute we were on top of a wave and no sea could be seen next in a valley with the sea rising almost to the sky, it was almost impossible to walk about. Everything had to be secured. I remember sitting in the canteen when cartons etc began sliding off the shelves and had to be packed away until the storm abated. After two days we turned North and gradually the weather improved, we were told our position was south of Cape Town.

Having left the UK in September 1941, it was now November 1941, we had been at sea for two months and possibly no one other than Winston Churchill knew where we would finally land. We approached Cape Town from the east, probably to convince any spies that we were travelling west. Our boat finally docked and dropped anchor at the quay side, not far from another very large and beautiful ship called the 'Westpoint.' Soon after docking the Officer IC troops gave permission for shore leave from 1 PM till midnight, this was met with loud cheers on deck. We soon realised this would be our first opportunity to wear our new tropical kit. With no thought of food both Doug. and I had fully dressed complete with pith helmet and ready to down the gangway as soon as possible. Going ashore was an exciting prospect. We felt very comfortable, the weather was perfect a pleasant warm and sunny day, we thought Cape Town had a perfect climate for a winter holiday. This time of the year is of course their summer. We had not even got to the end of the quay when a Rolls Royce stopped and a middle aged lady lowered the car window and asked if we had planned to go anywhere special, I looked at Doug and we both at the same time said 'no,' she immediately offered to show us around the Cape, which we gladly accepted. Getting into the car we were introduced to another lady who explained that they were sisters. The car was chauffeur driven and we were taken for a run, we saw the cable way to Table Mountain, They drove into the naval base at Simondstown, some time later we eventually drove up to a beautiful house on the beach at Muzenburg and were invited in.

The house was out of this world with every luxury, we were immediately served with drinks and other snacks, the sisters then asked what time we had to be back on board and suggested we stay for dinner and they would take us back to the ship in good time. They made great efforts to entertain us and we had a fabulous evening meal. In the cause of conversation we found out that they were of Dutch origin. They took the names and addresses of our parents and said they would write and tell them they had seen us and how well we looked. (When I eventually arrived home after the war the letter was shown to me and we realised that they were connected with a diamond mine in Johannesburg.) I am sorry to say that I can no longer trace the letter.

We eventually set sail again, it's now December 1941, once out of sight of land the boat turned and headed in an easterly direction and soon the weather began to get very hot but this was bearable due to a sea breeze, we also began sleeping out on the deck again. At night it was interesting to watch a phosphorus glow in the white foam created by the boat moving through the water. By day it was entertaining to watch the flying fish rising and skimming across the water. One day the American crew started to shout and scream to one another, we asked why. On the radio they had heard of the attack on Pearl Harbour and of course we eventually heard that the Japanese had declared war on the USA and Gt. Britain on 7th December 1941. News was also received that our battleships 'Repulse' and 'Prince Of Wales' had been sunk by the Japanese off Malaya on 11th. December 1941. The USA declared war on Japan and Germany 10th December 1941. We spent Christmas in the Indian Ocean with the traditional turkey and Christmas pudding. After several more days at sea, land again came in sight and as we sailed into the docks we were told it was Bombay. Soon after docking, we received instructions to pack all kit ready to land. Our immediate thoughts were confused, there was no war going on in India. Our kit was loaded onto vehicles and we set off to march into the centre of the city, we finally arrived at a barrack building that had been used by the regular resident British Army. We spent a week in Bombay which was very enjoyable after the boring months at sea. Life in Bombay seemed to be totally different from anywhere else in the world. Nowhere is there such extremes of livelihood, walking the streets it is possible to see the very rich in their beautiful and bright native dress to the other extreme, beggars and those that we called sand rats. I cannot recall why we gave them this name, but if they touched me it made me shudder, especially the women, quite often it was possible to see slime running down their legs. At night it was almost impossible to walk along the footpaths after a night out as the pathway was almost taken over by these people sleeping. Then next morning a vehicle normally used to collect refuse travels round the streets collecting the dead. These people get their food from hotels in the area. No food is thrown away, all leftovers are put into a container and placed outside the hotel, this fly ridden food is then quickly disposed of by beggars.

Our nights out were spent mostly at one particular night-club as the cinemas only showed Indian films which we could not understand. At the night-club there was a drawback, it was necessary to tip the waiter every time you called for a drink, if you didn't he would ignore any more requests, considering that his time was more profitable serving people who constantly tipped. The temperature at night in Bombay was noticeably warmer than expected, during the day duties would finish at lunch time, the afternoon would be spent either resting or light sports activity. But we were not free to go out until the evening.

We stayed in Bombay almost two weeks, after which we boarded a train to God knows where. We travelled for several days passing through Poona on the way. The most interesting part of this journey happened at the stations when the train stopped, all we had to do was shout through the window, "Char" and a Char Waller (Hindu for tea man) would fill our mugs with hot sweet tea for one anna. I cannot ever recall getting a drink of tea as good as that from a Char Waller. Travelling through India, one is again reminded of the extremely poor quality of life that most of the people have to endure. Most of the country consists of small dilapidated villages with mud huts in dusty open countryside whose residents seem to work on small plots of land. Our train journey ended on the 8th of January 1942. After a short walk we entered a large prefabricated building again in open countryside. It was filled with beds made from rough wood with medium thick type of rope lattice to lie on, they were very comfortable. The place was called Ahmednager. The countryside was devoid of vegetation, except for a few crops grown by the peasants with water being constantly drawn from wells by a bullock attached to a wooden pole to make him walk around the well in a circle to draw up the water. The river beds had dried up, we had been told that no rain had fallen here for seven years. The roads were no more than dust tracks. Our water came from large tanks erected on stilts to gravity feed our open air washing facilities and cookhouse. Soon after setting up the camp we were joined by a number of Hindu's, they set up their camp outside our perimeter, they called themselves our "followers". They fed from our scraps and left overs. For less than two Annas a week each, they cooked washed our clothes cleaned the building etc, some of the lads were even given a shave before getting out of bed in the morning. The Char Waller sat outside our billet 24 hours a day with his tea urn. It was rich pickings for him. We had a problem with a large bird called a Shiite Hawk which also lived off us. We collected our food from a service point outside the cook house and had to carry it a short distance to tables in the open but under a roof, during the short walk if you were not careful the hawks would swoop down and snatch the food from your mess tin. That was it, no way could you go back to the cookhouse for more. It was extremely hot in Ahmednager again the afternoon was spent relaxing, but at night it became very cold, so going to bed was enjoyable. We had no hot water for washing but the water from the overhead tanks to our ablution point was always warm from the unceasing heat of the day.

Evenings soon became very boring, nothing to do, no where to go. The Commanding Officer managed to make contact with a bus company and hired some buses. Anyone wishing to go out in the evening were then taken about six miles to an Indian bazaar. This was just a couple of rows of open shops, but at least it was a change of scenery for a few hours. One evening arrangements were made for an Indian illusionist to visit the camp. I particularly remember two tricks. First, he bent a steel bar with his neck. He asked for five lads from the audience, one to hold the bar at the centre, one end was placed against the seat of a chair held by the four men, the other end was placed at the hole of his neck. Holding the bar he asked the four men to push, push, the man in the middle was asked to move away, the Indian stood his ground and kept asking the four to push, push the bar eventually bent in the middle. The other trick had to be the Indian Rope Trick, which he performed outside just to prove he could do it. I still wonder to this day where that boy went to from the top of the rope.

Chapter IV

The Forgotten Army's Last Journey

Our stay in Ahmednager came to an end and we were on the move again. The train took us back to Bombay and we boarded an old coal burning ship called 'The Empress Of Asia', It was now Friday 23rd January 1942. We immediately set sail. The ship's crew moaned and complained about setting sail on a Friday, they said it was unlucky to set sail on this day. Again we were off to an unknown destination, the ship seemed to be heading in an easterly direction.

Twelve days later, we were in the war. At 10-30 am on the morning of the 4th of February 1942 our convoy was attacked by nine Japanese bombers, we had orders to go and stay below decks. I personally felt very scared, being at the mercy of the enemy and not a "Cat in hells chance" of being able to defend in any way but just sit there and wait for the inevitable. We could hear and feel the bombs exploding in the sea around us but luckily our boat had no direct hits. The bombing raid only lasted a short while. Sometime later we found out that we were about two days sail from Singapore and that the planes may have already been on a raid over the Island. For the rest of that day we continually scanned the horizon expecting to see more planes, non appeared, the night that followed was a very uneasy one.

Going on deck early next morning our ship was on its own. The rest of the convoy was out of sight. After breakfast it was announced that the stokers who were apparently foreigners had stolen rafts and left the ship during the night. We were now drifting, going nowhere, there was also a mine field to worry about. A request was made for volunteers to stoke the boilers. I personally do not believe in omens, and remembering what the sailors said about setting sail on a Friday. This day was the 5th of February 1942, exactly thirteen days from the day we set sail. At precisely 11-30 am we heard the drone of planes, we counted three sets of nine in formation, again we were ordered to go below. Soon we heard the bombs falling around the ship and then it seemed to heave and shudder there was a feeling of concussion, I thought my eardrums would burst, obviously the ship had been hit several times, we were of course unprotected and sitting ducks. My feelings were rather strange, there was no fright just extreme anger, at not being able to respond. An officer came down to our deck and said quite calmly, leave everything, we must abandon the ship immediately. There was no rush, just an orderly climb to the top deck, when I got there I saw men jumping overboard to join many others already in the water, planes were still overhead dropping their bombs. For some strange reason, although the ship was well and truly on fire I did not feel the urge to go over the side, I thought the sharks might get me then again I realised the bombs would have scared them off. I then noticed a naval ship steaming towards us and as it came closer I saw that it was a sloop called 'Yarrow.' Obviously Australian, without fear of any danger it came alongside our ship and its sailors shouted, "catch these ropes", which we tied to our ship's rail. I then shouted to the lads go down hand over hand or you will burn the skin off your hands. Strangely I was still in no hurry to get off myself. I turned round to see who was next, I had a terrible shock my Company Commander stood there, he had very little clothing on that was not burned, his skin was blue and hanging off his arms and body in sheets, for a moment I lost my nerve and said "no Sir you can't go down the rope". Eventually we found some canvas and made a sort of stretcher to lower him onto the sloop. When eventually I landed on the sloop's deck I turned and looked at the 'Asia,' it was burning from stem to stern and I immediately thought of the lovely camera I had left with all my kit. I then suddenly realised that the Jap. planes had gone, obviously thinking they had finished us off. There was a state of chaos on the deck of the sloop, the crew were running around trying to pick our men up out of the sea, we who had land-ed on their deck sat down trying to keep out of the way, there were loads of empty anti aircraft shells rolling around, they had obviously been firing at the Jap. planes, anyone who looked to be dead was left in the sea. We never found out how many men were killed in the attack on the ship, although I heard that our Commanding Officer died two days later. I was in the war and had experienced a good christening. When I eventually reached dry land the first person I saw was the Colonel of our regiment walking along the sea front. He was very dishevelled and barefoot. He called us together and said come on lads follow me. We arranged ourselves in marching order and marched off, civilians stared at us as we passed by, some of us with clothes on, some without, others had sailor's clothes. Some even in civvies what a sight, but we held our heads high. Such was the British bulldog spirit. We eventually arrived at an empty school room I noticed the outside was full of shrapnel holes, in fact many buildings looked rather battered, as we passed them by.

The following two days were spent re equipping. Each morning at about 11-30 am we had an air raid of 27 bombers. There was no R.A.F to counter attack we had been told they had already left the Island. In fact the roads around the docks were littered with abandoned cars, left by civilians who had left all their belongings and homes to quickly board any ship that was prepared to take them off the Island. We understood that the Japanese had now reached Johore, which was just across the causeway from the Island. Perhaps I could mention here that Singapore is very densely populated and about 17 by 15 miles in size.

On the 7th of February we took up positions along the Buket Timah Road which runs to the causeway and Johore, to wait for the enemy. They invaded on the 8th of February, but not from the causeway, our engineers had blown it up. We dug shallow slit trenches for protection from mortar bombs, but they were of little use as we had to move around to deal with pockets of resistance. We were killing about five Japs. to one of ours, but as fast as we shot one another took his place. It was very difficult to know exactly where they were due to the rather dense vegetation in that area. We also had a very large rubber plantation between them and us. In one sortie a Jap had managed to climb a tree very close during the night, and soon after daylight he started sniping, he must have killed several of our lads. It's a well-known fact that the Scots are good fighters, I, for added protection decided to join up with a party of three named McGuire, Mc Leod and Ewing, they were happy to let me go along with them, on hunting for Japanese expeditions. Of course we went in search of the one in the tree and eventually saw him, he saw us at the same time and moved behind the trunk to shield himself from attack, we just split up, two one way, two the other. I emptied a complete magazine into his body, I am sure he was dead when we left him. We also became ruthless with civilians riding their cycles along the road towards the enemy, we found that after a short while we experienced some very accurate direct mortar bombing. Afterwards any civilian going in the direction of the enemy was shot. At night the sky was lit by the explosions of shells from our artillery, this with the continuous lightning that goes on in this part of the world, and the constant pounding and a slushing noise of the very large shells passing overhead from our cannons at Black Amati together with mortar bombs exploding amongst us gave us no respite. I cannot recall having a full nights rest during the whole time in action. Every day at the same time each morning we would hear the Jap planes coming, dive into slit trenches and watch them come in formation and complete freedom. there was no RAF to engage them. If they released any bombs before they came overhead we hoped they would miss us, but those leaving the planes when overhead did not bother us. The bombs they used were a type of Anti Personnel bomb which exploded scattering shrapnel outwards over a wide area, there was no crater. Anyone above ground would not stand a chance and there was no time to bury the dead. In forty-eight hours a body would be crawling with maggots. The flies in Singapore laid a live maggot not an egg which immediately attacked wounds went up the nose and into the mouth. Within a few days there would be nothing left but a skeleton, the scalp and hair, the stench was terrible. I mention these happenings in a matter of fact way for a very good reason and which is very difficult to explain. My feelings in general began to change from the day we were bombed on board ship, the sight of our men being killed created a feeling of deep anger, as the days progressed it seemed to develop into a sort of temporary madness, fear seemed to desert me, and I had no problem killing little young Japanese soldiers, in fact after killing I could put my boot into his face and grind it. I remember one night in particular we happened to be resting in an open area close to a rubber planters house, it was empty as the owners had left in a hurry some days earlier. During the night we sustained heavy mortar fire, several of our men had been killed and an Officer was very badly injured. Next morning I was sure we had been surrounded during the night. Realising that we should move out as quickly as possible I began going round the men trying to rouse them so that we could leave in one body, I had very little response, we'd had very little rest during the past four days, I began kicking them to try and get them on their feet, still they did not move. I picked up a Bren Gun and shouted: "I'll shift you, you buggers," and it's true I was going to shoot them. Someone quickly snatched the gun from my hands and shouted, "What the effing hell mate." Again I suddenly seemed to realise my state of madness. We then quickly made plans to leave and virtually retreat. We prepared our weapons in readiness to charge across an open space and through the Japanese line. I picked up the Bren Gun, (light machine gun) made sure the magazine was fully charged, Douglas was with me this time, I told him to get right behind me. We could not take the Officer he was too wounded. We decided to spray the undergrowth immediately in front of us beyond the clearing and hope to get through. When we got on our feet someone shouted go. I have never run so fast in my life firing as I went. Douglas and I reached the rubber plantation safely, I never found out if and how many did not make it, I only remember we ran so fast I did not see a single Japanese. We continued to run and run until we came to a battery of our own artillery and someone shouted to us, "Where the effing hell are you lot going to?" Which again brought us back to our senses, the following day we joined another group and took up a new position the other side of the main road but in the rear of the previous one. We were now beginning to realise that we were in retreat and heavily outnumbered. The bombardment continued from the land and the air. Thick palls of black smoke filled the air over the Island. Oil tanks were blown up. Many civilians had already been killed due to the dense population. Mains water had been cut from the mainland. Rivers had been infected and I had used some water from a river a few days earlier. My face started to itch and I could not resist scratching it, soon it became very sore. Then someone said have you seen your face and produced a mirror, I had a shock, it was covered in big black sores, what a mess. An Officer arranged for someone to run me into town to a chemist who gave me some ointment to apply. He advised me to get further treatment, but I had to return to action but again instructed to go back to town where I could get further treatment and at the same time take up the duty of guarding Singapore railway station, which was now completely deserted. Here I was joined by several other injured men. We spent some of our time in the bar serving one another drinks, thinking why should we let the Japs have it. We disposed of bottles of Gin etc. by placing them on a wall and using them for rifle practice. Three days later on Sunday 15th of February 1942 we were forced to capitulate. At that moment in time my feelings were mixed, we had been told to fight to the last man. From our point of view our army had not been beaten, there was a feeling of relief that the fighting had stopped. For me the war was over and I was a prisoner of war. What would they do with us. All the training and expense, the travelling had been a waste of time. At that moment I had nothing but hate for Winston Churchill, realising he had sacrificed the whole of the 18th Division. The Island was as good lost before we arrived. We had travelled in ships almost all over the world since leaving the UK. in September 1941, presumably to reinforce our army in North Africa and join the newly formed 8th Army to fight the Germans led by General Rommel. For some unknown reason the mission was aborted and we spent weeks 'kicking our heels' in India, as a result became known as The Forgotten Army. The realisation and frustration, that millions of pounds had been spent assembling, training and equipping, a highly technical and mechanised unit, had been to no avail. Then to find that ultimately, every man was issued with nothing more than a rifle each and expected to get on with it, after having been dumped in a territory which had already been almost overrun by the enemy.

I am sure that the details of this disaster was evidently 'swept under the carpet,' as neither Churchill or his generals, as far as I am aware, were asked to answer for this military 'cock up.' Which ultimately resulted in the wastage and loss of life of many thousands of my comrades.

Chapter V

We Surrender

Singapore was in ruins, dense clouds of smoke filled the sky, buildings riddled with shrapnel holes, the streets littered with abandoned cars and other vehicles together with army vehicles. The water supply piped from the mainland had been cut off, the civilian population of this densely packed Island had suffered a severe battering. This we believe was the main reason why General Percival made the decision to surrender. Soon after capitulation the Japanese arrived and we were ordered to hand over all weapons and ammunition which we stacked in a pile. My thoughts were at that point in time. 'How could we have been beaten by these silly looking little men in scruffy uniforms and the funniest of rubber boots with a cleft big toe.' (They were black canvas and rubber with the big toe in its own compartment from the rest of the foot.) They then ordered us to march off to join several hundred other prisoners, we looked a very dejected lot of men, we only had what we stood up in.

After a night lying around in an open piece of ground an officer told us we had got to move off to march to a place called Changi, which was about sixteen miles north of the town. I had not eaten since noon the previous day. As we set off mid morning the heat was intense and there was not much water in my bottle. As we passed through the streets traces of the battle could be seen. Abandoned lorries cars, motor cycles and other debris littered the streets. The Chinese and Malays lined the streets to watch us pass. The Chinese, bless them took their lives into their hands as we passed by several ran into the road to offer food and drink which we gladly accepted. Mile after mile we trudged in the terrible heat, even the Jap guards were lagging behind occasionally. Passing out of the town we noticed a spiked fence and on each spike was impaled the head of a Chinese civilian. I counted many heads along the route and tried to concentrate on my own situation, I resisted drinking from my water bottle, it was sheer torture, I just allowed myself to wet my lips and tongue, to have had a drink would have been a disaster, and I would not have been able to stop. It just acts like a drug in that heat.

We eventually arrived at Changi in the early evening, worn out and very unhappy. I found Changi to be a magnificent strip of country, bounded on two sides by the sea. The buildings, now in a state of ruin, and scattered over a wide area had been the palatial barracks and officer's messes of a well-known British Regiment. Some of the buildings had been three storeys, and had sustained severe shell damage, there was no running water or electricity. It was decided that all troops would have to live in the open and any building that could be used would be for officers and a medical centre. But most important of all, a place to store the several trucks of food which someone with hindsight had managed to load and bring to Changi. Whilst being confined to Changi we saw very little of the I.J.A, (Imperial Japanese Army). All instructions had to be carried out by our officers. The following days were spent building cook houses digging latrines, establishing and organising a medical centre for the wounded. I had been ordered to attend daily for treatment to my face which had now deteriorated to large black scabs of puss. Myself and several others managed to chop branches off several small trees which we used to erect a cover to which we attached our ground sheets, under which we slept and sheltered from the rain. We also found it necessary to construct carts to move food and other equipment around the camp. We managed to convert several damaged vehicles by removing all unnecessary structure to lighten them as we were not allowed any fuel for the engines. It was a very strange sight to see these vehicles being dragged around the camp with a piece of rope to pull them by several men.

About a week after being taken prisoner the Nips ordered us to line the roads running through Changi to enable their high ranking officers to inspect and gloat over their capture of many thousands of British,Australian,Indian and Gurkha troops. It was repeated the following day for the benefit of the Japanese navy. Soon after this humiliating incident parties of men were being taken back to the city to work on clearing up operations. I could not go because of my ulcerated face, medical supplies were severely restricted and thus it was not showing any signs of clearing up. Those returning to Changi for any reason gave us news that their living conditions in town were much better, they lived in huts and whilst out on working parties they found it possible to nick food from the docks and sneak it back into camp, where quite a lot of bartering went on with all the stuff they had managed to nick and secretly hide away in a vehicle or any equipment they used. All abandoned vehicles, cars, military, guns etc., were being taken to the docks and loaded onto ships for Japan. One of the worst and distressing jobs involved scouting around the undergrowth for bodies to bury, which would now be skeletons. There were hundreds and the work went on for weeks.

The sanitation in Changi was now getting awful, what with the lack of sufficient water, and fly infested latrines, we began to realise what a struggle our prison life was going to be. Our food rations now consisted of very small amounts of tinned meat and rice. On many occasions during these early days of captivity the thought of escape came into our minds but was immediately dismissed as it was considered to be out of the question as we were thousands of miles both by land jungle and sea from any allied troops. Recapture would mean instant death probably beheaded with the sword, what a thought? Natives without doubt would inform as although small there was a price on our heads, they would not hesitate for the money. News had also filtered through to us that all Allied women and children in Singapore had been collected together and forced to walk the sixteen miles to Changi gaol. They were forced to carry all clothing, and push prams. After the easy life they had lead, walking this distance in the tropical heat, they would without doubt struggle, and probably collapse on their journey. This shows the sheer brutality of the I.J.A. remembering all the vehicles and buses left choking the streets.

During the many days that followed, those of us left in Changi had very little to occupy our minds, there were the usual chores of keeping the area reasonably tidy also trying to get any news of what was going on in the outside world, most often it was all rumour. At night fires would be lit to cook the bits of food obtained from various sources, we would sit around the fire and visualise what a tasty meal would be like. In the mornings we would run down towards the sea as just off the shore we found many coconut trees growing loaded with coconuts but as the trees were about 30 to 40 feet high the nuts were out of reach. they would only fall to the ground when brown and ripe, we usually found a few each morning. The coconut on the tree is green and after forming is about the size of a very large water melon but oval in shape. Beneath the outer tough smooth cover there is a two and a half inch layer of fibre and about two pints of sweet coconut juice. As the nut forms and hardens inside the fibre the juice helps to grow the white flesh of the nut and reduces in content as the flesh grows, when ripe the whole thing turns brown and falls to the ground. We have all seen how trained monkeys have run up these trees and twisted the nut round and round until it falls. Occasionally we were able to persuade a local native to climb the trees with his jungle knife and chop a few down, he would then chop off the end of the green casing and several of us would sample a good long drink of the cool sweet juice.

The days at Changi were long and I was beginning to get fed up, the spare European food had now been used up and we now lived on rice and boiled green vegetables, just enough to keep us alive. The medics have been using a tablet ground to powder on my face and thankfully the scabs are going leaving my face covered in brown marks where they had been. It still looked a mess. We are all now loosing weight and disease is taking its toll. Dysentery, malnutrition and other problems are increasing the death rate. Have started a burial party and they are working all day and every day. There were still in the region of 20 to 30 thousand prisoners at that time still in Changi. (At this point it would be worth mentioning that my parents were notified on the 26th March 1942 that I was reported as missing in Malaya. This would be the first indication of where I was since leaving England in 1941, except of course they did get a letter from the people who entertained me in Cape Town.)

In May 1942, having been a prisoner for three months I was told that I would be joining a party of six hundred men to work in Singapore. What a relief as I knew that more food would be available and I had heard that the men working in the City were getting paid, but not looking forward to the journey as I knew we had to walk back the sixteen miles in the heat and now not as fit as when we first came here. At 8 am on the morning of 14th May 1942 I lined up with the other men in our party. I should mention here that I had lost touch with Douglas. He had been sent on another party some weeks earlier and it transpired that I was never to set eyes on him again. For the march I had jettisoned anything that would not be of immediate use, to help me make the journey. We set off and soon passing by Changi gaol, the women could be seen waving their hankies to us through the grills of the windows, our hearts went out to them and we wondered how they were being treated. The march was heavy going, the heat intense and I began to get dizzy spells but resisted drinking from my water bottle. I had planned to not allow myself a drink until after approximately 12 miles. After about 8 miles several of the weaker ones began to collapse at the roadside. We later found out that all of them had been picked up and brought in to join us. The heat was giving us hell and about 2 pm we stopped for one hour. Myself and several other lads found a tree and fell exhausted under it. After a while recovering I decided to eat my two rice balls and bit of dried fish with a very small drink of water. The short break went all too quickly and we set off again, the heat now more intense as it was mid afternoon. I was soon soaked in sweat which dripped from my body constantly, it was hell.

My back pack was cutting into my shoulder through the thin khaki drill shirt. We were allowed to halt again with about 5 miles to go, close to some shops. Whilst the guards were nowhere near we sneaked into the shops for anything they had. It was too good to miss. I was given some bananas. Once again the local Chinese had been very kind to us. After half an hour we set off again and the blast furnace heat was beginning to cool as the sun began to sink towards the horizon, eventually we arrived at River Valley Road camp, but learnt that we had to go to another camp in Havelock Road which was close by. Our first sight of this camp was rather disappointing. It consisted of a dozen huts in swampy ground and very long grass. There were no washing facilities and no cook house. It had apparently been a refugee camp which had been built by the local authority many months earlier for use by the native population in case they were bombed out of there homes. The huts had a wood platform about seven feet wide and about two feet six inches from the earthen floor and running the full length of the hut with a six foot gangway in the centre. A further platform had been erected above about seven feet from the floor with ladders every few feet to enable us to climb to the upper deck. All four decks were to be our living and sleeping quarters for the next six months. We were packed like sardines with about 2 feet 9 inches of space for each man. The huts were about 100 metres long with a wood framework covered with what was called 'atap.' (Atap is made from a form of palm leaf folded over a 3 foot length of split bamboo and sort of stitched and fastened tile fashion over the roof and sides) There were no doors or windows, just a large opening at each end of the hut, they looked just like a barn for animals, we were being treated no better.

Too tired to bother much we were herded into the huts, I opted for a space on the upper deck just inside on the right and was joined by other men, two of whom became firm friends, I had not known them until this moment. Our officers occupied the next hut to ours, they were a little better off there was no upper deck and they had their collapsible portable beds to sleep on and a mosquito net. That evening the cooks somehow managed to prepare a meal of rice and vegetables mostly greens and a little sweet potato, a drink consisted of a mug of boiled water. After which we dropped off to sleep completely exhausted.

The following morning waiting for the Japs to arrive was spent exploring the camp. There were two entrances, one of which bridged a narrow river into a large open shed which housed all the vehicles which I understood would be used in connection with our work. Beyond the MT shed I noticed a street and shops, these shops were to become very valuable to me, but the reason will become apparent later. Walking in the long grass in an open space beyond the officer's hut I had quite a shock. A clothed skeleton lay there with nothing left but his scalp and hair, I think it had been a civilian man, walking away with a shudder, I was reminded of this bloody war

We soon found out how we were expected to be occupied. Quite a number of men were lucky to be chosen to drive the vehicles, three others joined him to assist loading and unloading, this was the crew for each truck. The rest of us, (the unlucky ones) were split up into groups of six, we had to use carts which we loaded and pulled ourselves. We were lucky in this respect, whereas a Nip travelled as passenger in the trucks, we would be in a convoy of several carts with one Nip, he could not watch all of us, so it was easy to take the occasional opportunity to slip into a shop etc. on our travels. It did not take many days for the men to start the "rackets". Now the word racket in our camp meant simply finding a method of extracting money from one another by buying and selling mainly items of food and anything else we were able to scrounge, beg or steal whilst out on working parties. Although we were getting just a little more food than we got in Changi it was still quite inadequate to maintain fitness. The causeway had now been repaired and working parties travelling to the mainland found pineapples growing just off the road, it was easy for them to pick a few on the way back and sell them once back in camp. This is how the rackets first started. Soon a piece of ground was allocated where men could light a fire to make tea, coffee, cocoa, or fry up anything they had managed to buy or steal during the day. Empty ten gallon petrol cans were brought into use for boiling the tea or coffee. At night the tea and coffee sellers would make a brew in their petrol cans and come round the huts shouting "hot sweet tea or coffee, five cents a mug," they always sold out. I should also mention that on working parties we were being paid fifteen cents a day to work, not much, but better than nothing, at least it was a little to help supplement our meagre food ration. The most popular buy to go with a meal was an egg and these were in plentiful supply from a shop we passed just before entering our camp. Beautiful large duck eggs. I then had a brain wave. My chance came one day whilst working in the MT. shed. I took the chance to nip across the road to speak to the Chinese shop owner to try and do a deal. He agreed to supply me with eggs at five cents each providing I bought at least twelve dozen each time. That night I discussed the possibilities with my two new friends Ken and Ray. Pooling our resources we could only raise two dollars fifty cents. Ray was batman to a Captain Bancroft and suggested asking his Officer if he would like to make up the difference of five dollars until we could pay him back, he agreed on the understanding that he had his eggs at cost price, we agreed whole heartedly. The biggest problem was how to get the eggs into camp. First we obtained two empty petrol tins these measured about ten inches square by about fifteen inches deep, I fitted wire to act as carrying handles, these would hold the twelve dozen eggs we planned to buy. The plan of action was then worked out. The quickest way to and from the shop was to get past the guard at the entrance to the MT shed, which meant a quick dash over the narrow river bridge and into the MT shed and out of sight of the guard. I agreed to be the one to chance it and collect the eggs, but the big problem was how to distract the guards attention, to enable me to run across the bridge and into the shed, it was decided that Ray with two other men would stroll along towards the Jap looking at snaps of their wives etc, once the Jap was interested they would stand around him to obstruct his view, after all they were very short, I would be somewhere behind them watching and walking by, then at the right moment suddenly change direction, nip past them over the bridge and into the shed. I would then casually walk across the road to the shop to buy the eggs. Returning I would wait under cover of the shed until another group engaged the Jap with something else so that I could then slip back into camp. The first effort was a complete success. We sold the eggs at ten cents each, either raw or boiled. This rather dangerous exercise could not be carried out too often as we had to ensure that guard was a different man on each occasion. We eventually ran out of luck, on this occasion I had the eggs and as I came over the bridge he somehow saw me, he raised his rifle and motioned me to go to him. He made me stand there with him until relieved, when I was marched back to the guard room. They took the eggs from me, stood me to attention outside, a senior guard, a hancho, (corporal in our rank,) came outside towards me, I wondered what was going to happen to me. He uttered the words: "Canero, buggero, English soldier no good," struck me four times across both sides of my face with his hands and all his might. (The uttering canero, buggero are sort of swear words they used when cursing us). This treatment to prisoners happened regularly and was considered to be a mild form of punishment. This same type of punishment was also used on their own soldiers. I was left to stand to attention outside the guard hut for the rest of the day in the tropical heat, this experience turned out to be worse than the corporal punishment. the fact that I could not move a limb was agony in the intense heat, at any moment with my head swimming I felt I was going to collapse to the ground, but gritting my teeth I overcame the feeling and found that if I rocked a little I could move my weight first to one leg and then the other it seemed to help me to concentrate in my predicament. Had I collapsed they would have come outside and repeated the punishment. Eventually evening arrived and they told me in pigeon English to return to my hut for "Tenco." (The evening count of prisoners.) After which we had our evening meal of rice and veg. Sitting in our hut afterwards I discussed the situation. It seemed that the egg business was finished, and could not be risked again, the eggs were still with our guards and presumably lost. Their value in money upset me I said, "I am going to have a go at getting them back," my mates said, "you're bloody mad," I said "I probably am but I'm still going."I rose and sauntered towards the guard hut with some apprehension wondering what to say, reaching the hut I felt a little lucky, one of the Japs came outside walking up to him I bowed, saluted and said rubbing my stomach "English soldiers mishi mishi (Japanese for food) very good help work" and then pointing towards the hut, said "Eggs me have" and then pointing to myself hoping that he understood. He thought for a few moments then laughed his head off, suddenly he came up to me drew back his arm and punched me at the side of my face, he did this six times with alternate arms, how I continued to stand I will never know. He then indicated me to wait, went into hut and returned with the two containers of eggs, giving them to me he said, "OK take very good mishi mishi." My mates had a shock when they saw me on my return with the eggs, but they were very pleased. I said "Yes but at a price," then telling what had happened.

The month was now July 1942 we have been in captivity for five months, our clothes are now getting very ragged and rotting due to being constantly wet with perspiration, As stated previously we now only have one set of clothes, we give them a rinse in water and put them back on, we have no soap left, some men have already discarded worn out boots and now wear own made wooden clop clops. We are getting very thin, dysentery, dengue fever and other problems are a constant menace, there are no medical supplies and the medical officer is having terrible problems with the sick. The change in diet effects the body in all sorts of ways. I seem to remember it was about this time that my testicles began to itch, and found that many other men were experiencing the same problem. It was impossible not to scratch, in doing so there was some relief and at the same time, perhaps should not mention I had a strange feeling of pleasure which was almost impossible to resist. During the night it would get worse, I would wake up finding myself scratching away. Eventually the skin broke and became infected, the irritation stopped as the testicles became very sore and soon developed into balls of discharging puss. We could only walk with our legs open to stop the testicles rubbing on the inside of our legs. It looked really funny, but it wasn't. I heard that some men had to have them taken off, again I was lucky as by somehow keeping clean the problem eventually cleared up.

One day returning from a working party every man was given a piece of paper, on it was a statement which read " I promise not try escape" followed by a place for a signature. The officers also had the same request. Now it is well known that it's a prisoner of war's responsibility to try to escape. So we all refused to sign it, as it was against international laws. Because we would not sign we were all marched off to an open space surrounded by a wire fence like a tennis court. we were herded into this space to be followed by men from another camp. There were, I was told about seventeen thousand men being crowded into a space that would take only about one thousand, it would be impossible to lie down. The Japs posted sentries all around us with machine guns trained on us. We all thought this was going to be our last day of life. I immediately thought of my family at home in England and prayed for a painless end. It did not happen but was torture for two whole days, we did get some food but very little and a small amount of water, but had to urinate etc. on the spot where we were, so you can imagine our situation after two days, the stench was vile, if something did not happen quickly we would all be dead anyway from disease. Thank God we were given permission to sign by senior officers but also told that the promise need not be kept as it was obtained under duress. We then were given orders to return to our camp and resume our daily work routine. Life again settled down to the usual camp fires at night where we sit and talk about food and other things. Rumours would be passed on one to another about some one who had a secret radio. One rather amusing rumour went round that the Russians were in Greece, we wondered why the Russians were in Greece. The truth eventually came to light when some one said what was really overheard was "That the rations had been increased."

August and September came and went, we had built a road through the camp, a small hut was converted to a church, the Padre and myself carried out communion and other services which were always very well attended. Being a trained alter server I was able to assist the Padre to carry out all services without the use of prayer books. We used small rice balls to act as the bread and a brew of cold tea as wine. During a service the Shinto Japs would stand at the entrance sneering. We eventually found out that the Japanese were mainly Shinto's, but a small number practised Christianity. But what was more strange, we found that the Christians ill-treated us worse than the Shinto's. News was also coming in that the Sikhs, Punjabs and Gurkhas who were part of our army in Malaya had been subjected to some severe punishment in an attempt to get them to change sides. We eventually found that the Sikh's gave in and within days our Jap guards were replaced by Sikh's, they treated us worse than the Japs, obviously to curry favour. People at home may not be aware of these facts, especially when it is realised how this country welcomes their immigrants with open arms. At the end of September we received a very pleasant surprise as we were told that some Red Cross parcels had arrived. Overjoyed we waited patiently for them to be split and shared. We also had news that we were soon to move somewhere else. We put it out of our minds to think about the food and perhaps clothing in the food parcels. We finally received a few tins of food which went to the cookhouse as it was felt that this was the best way to distribute it. The Japs only gave us part of the shipment saying we would receive the rest when we arrived at our new destination.

Chapter VI

Journey To The Hell Camps

It is now October 1942 and having packed our few belongings we set off from Havelock Road camp to walk the short distance to Singapore railway station, it was about four o'clock in the afternoon, still very hot and tiring. On arrival at the station we were entrained straight away in enclosed steel wagons with a sliding door in the centre, every wagon had to take thirty-two men, including officers. We were piled in irrespective of rank, there were that many in each truck it would be impossible to lie down; in fact with thirty-two in each truck we would have to take it in turns to even sit down. We thought maybe this was a good sign that we would not be travelling far under these conditions. Our hopes were short lived, the train crossed the Island and over the causeway into Johore, then stopped. Someone asked the Malayan guard where we were bound for as he passed by, "you are all going to Thailand" he said, "eight hundred miles- four days and four nights!" We all looked at one another, four days and four nights in this steel furnace, it's impossible in this tropical heat, however, it was true.

The engine took on water and blew its whistle, with a snatch and lurch the train moved off. We were all thrown on top of one another at the rear of the wagon. The wagons being loose coupled could not move off smoothly and as each coupling tightened the wagon would be snatched forward throwing us off our feet and on top of one another, there was nothing to hold on to. This happened every time we stopped and very often when moving, as the train accelerated and decelerated, the wagons would bang into one another even sitting to rest was almost impossible. The first night was bearable for a while but as the temperature dropped it went quite cold and we struggled to get away from the draughty doorway, whereas during the day we had to take it in turns be close to the door, the intense tropical heat turned the metal roof and sides into an oven. We had to remove all clothing except a loin cloth or shorts and let the perspiration drip from our bodies, how we withstood those terrible four days I will never know. We were not allowed off the train to toilet, luckily most of the country we passed through was jungle, but anyone who happened to be watching the train as it passed by would have without doubt seen strange parts of mens anatomy hanging out of the wagon doorways. We did not even get a drop of water for a wash during the whole journey. the stench in the wagons was sickening. Hour after hour the train trundled on, no one had the energy to even speak it was sheer misery. I prayed that I would survive the journey, I am sure the Japs hoped that none of us would. The only respite from the steel ovens occurred when the train stopped at various stations when a drum of rice and some watery stew, or stinking dried fish was issued to us as we queued in a long line waiting to be served. The food was very poor and only just enough to keep us alive.

The nightmare of this journey slowly continued, day after day as our train load of misery slowly made its way up the Malay Peninsular and eventually we entered Thailand and out of the jungle, passing through Thai. villages where people tried to get to the train when we stopped in order to try to buy clothing and blankets from us. At that time Thailand was very short of manufactured goods. Some of our men were able to get ten dollars for the odd blanket. Many of us could not resist the temptation to sell something. At least the money would buy some extra food. The officers made every effort to stop the troops selling their kit, which might be needed later on but it seemed useless as money was more valuable than clothes. Of course all bartering had to be done out of sight of the Japs. I only had one blanket, a ground sheet and what I stood up in, having already ditched everything else which I felt I could not carry. So I was not in any position to sell anything.

We eventually arrived at a station called Bampong in the early morning of the thirteenth of October. A very dirty and tired body of troops alighted from the train and after a short march another shock awaited us. We arrived at a camp consisting of about eight very badly constructed huts, but the biggest shock was that some of them were literally under water. To make matters worse, my two pals and myself found ourselves in one of them. The huts were the usual form, two platforms, one each side of the hut about two feet six inches from the earthen floor, but we had to wade through at least two feet of water to get on them, the water was literally a few inches below were we were going to sleep. Apparently a river close by had burst its banks. The officers complained but the Japs said it's only a transit camp and we would only be here for a few days. They seemed to think that prisoners of war would not mind sleeping in water, or having to wade up to their knees every time they wished to visit the latrine, after such a dreadful rail journey. My thoughts at this time were, it was bad enough in Singapore, but life there was a luxury compared with our present situation. Water was overflowing into the latrines which themselves overflowed bringing the filth into the huts the stench was terrible. The nights that followed were a misery, we could not sleep due to loud croaking of large frogs, they were everywhere.

We were told here that we were going to build a railway through the jungle all the way to India, again my thoughts were not very positive. I am thinking it will never be completed we will all die in the process. We were also told that there was a very long march in front of us.

Three days later at dawn we lined up on the road ready for the next stage of our journey, knowing that it was going to be life threatening, the officers have had to discard most of their kit as each man could only take that which he could carry. I noticed that some men were going to try and carry weights far in excess of the normal army standard for marching. As stated previously I only had what I stood up in, plus one blanket, a ground sheet, towel, and eating utensils, these were placed in a haversack to which I attached the blanket and ground sheet, all to be carried as a shoulder pack, my arms free to assist a steady walk. We were permitted a ten minute rest in every hour. The first three hours went quite well considering our weakness through lack of proper food, then as the temperature began to get unbearable I noticed a man here and there begin to drop something he was carrying to lighten his load. Having not done any considerable walking for some months, my legs and more so my feet were becoming quite painful. My shirt and shorts had already become saturated. About mid day we stopped, thank god, to eat the rice and a piece of dried fish which had been issued that morning after breakfast to pack in our mess tins. We tried to find out from our guards how far we had to go, I don't think they really knew as all sorts of miles were being quoted.

At this point of my epistle I feel that I should say something about our captors having now spent about eight months with them. We have been involved with both Japanese and Koreans acting as guards. Sometime after capture the Japanese left us and were replaced by Koreans. Somehow we found out that way back in their history the Koreans had disgraced the nation and as a result were not allowed to fight for Japan. This in context is, in their eyes, a disgrace. So their only job involved acting as guards of prisoners of war. We also soon learned that both Japanese and Koreans preferred to be called Niponese rather than Japanese as they came from Nipon. They also referred to some one called Tojo as their leader. In fact when speaking to us about leaders, they always said "Tojo number one, Churchill number two," meaning that Tojo was the better man. Most of them were of Shinto religion with a few Christians, but every morning at sunrise all had to stand outside their billet in a line facing east, take off any headgear, bow and say six words of prayer, bow again then go back inside. We used to have quite a laugh to ourselves about it. To us the words sounded like, "We want no more rice bust." Not true of course, but that's what it sounded like. To continue I shall now refer to our captors as "the Nips."

The break for food soon ended, at least we had stopped for about one hour at which point were urged to get up and be on our way. My legs felt heavy and like jelly, shutting the pain out I struggled to get on the move and after a while the pain eased off, the heat was sapping my strength, we tried to keep together but as the afternoon wore on some of the men began to drop behind, myself and several others kept close together and tried to carry on a conversation to shut out the misery of it all. I am sure that my guardian angel was helping me to carry on as during those next few hours men were falling out at the side of the road regularly, to the extent that the column of men had broken up to groups of stragglers. Thankfully the Chinese in the villages we passed through took pity on us and handed out drinks and fruit as we passed them, the Nips were also feeling the heat and beginning to struggle as they did nothing to stop the Chinese from helping us. Hour after hour we marched, the early evening arrived and we were still without any sign of stopping. Every time we stopped a few more men refused or were not able to carry on, they had reached a stage were they could not have cared less what happened to them. I think it was about seven o'clock when we reached a camp and we all dropped to the ground where we stood. Eventually we moved into the huts and soon were issued with a meal of rice and vegetable stew. We found a hose pipe and sprayed each other there were no other facilities, at least it was very enjoyable. The stragglers had to be brought in by trucks, it was about ten o'clock before all had been brought in. By this time most of the men were already asleep, without a thought of what tomorrow would bring.

Next morning our medical officer complained to the Nips that if help was not given by way of providing some transport to carry some of the kit and men who were by now in no fit condition to walk, due to swollen and sore feet, some could not even get their boots on. We knew they were trying to demoralise us, after all empty trucks had been passing us constantly on the road the previous day, they finally relented and provided several for some kit and anyone in no fit condition to walk. Again it was quite early when we set off, although we were tired from the previous day, the first few hours went without a problem, then suddenly a man fell to the ground in front of us, we lifted him to the side of the road and the Nips signalled us to leave him and carry on, before long as the heat of the day increased our weak and exhausted bodies began to submit to the agony of it all. Soon more men began to fall down with sheer exhaustion, it seemed as though the heat and loss of body fluid seemed to stifle breathing, I noticed it but was, luckily able to plod on but at a slower pace. It was noticeable the column began to string out and become longer and longer. The Nips were getting frustrated and began kicking and swearing at the men who were falling out. Lunch time finally arrived and we dragged ourselves to the side of the road which was now no more than a dust track and consumed what little food we had. It was promised that we would be able to refill our water bottles at this point but no water arrived. When we started off again local natives came from their huts again to bring water and the odd bit of fruit for which we were very thankful. The heat seemed to be more intense that afternoon. I again personally resisted drinking but just wet my tongue and face and it enabled me to carry on, although by now both my friends and I were near the back of the column. The guards were also, although only carrying rifles beginning to be showing signs of exhaustion and extending the hourly stops to fifteen minutes and sometimes more. Four o'clock came and someone said we had again covered over twenty miles since the dawn start. The biggest problem was not knowing exactly where we were going and how far we had to walk, this was the second day in the early evening and still no sign of any camp. I felt very light headed, my legs did not belong to me and we had to keep stopping for a rest, the guards began to get frustrated and annoyed as they were in no position to control us, the column had now extended over a great distance. We all looked a pitiful sight, badly sunburnt covered in dust and sweat sodden shirts and shorts. How we eventually reached the camp which was called Kanchanburi I will never know, it was about seven o'clock in the evening. We all dropped to the ground with relief and it was some time later we heard that one of our party had died of sheer exhaustion on the route. This was to be the first of many. It was ten o'clock that night before every one in the column managed to get off the road and into the camp. We were told that we had covered over fifty kilometres in the last two days. We were all suffering from complete exhaustion, sore and swollen feet, several hundred too ill to continue.

Our officers, who were in the same state realised that it would be impossible to continue marching the following day if we were going to survive, decided to ask for an interview with the head man of the I.J.A.(Imperial Japanese Army) to request one full days rest. The request was refused, the reason was that another thousand troops were following and we would have to leave the camp before they could come in. The officers again argued the impossibility of the situation and stressed that if we carried on no one would be left to work at the other end. The I.J.A. after coming round the camp to look at us decided to finally agree to one day of rest.

The huts and meals at Kanchanburi were much better than at anytime since we left Singapore, in fact it was a very good hospital camp. The day's rest and better food made us all feel some what refreshed. During the days rest the word passed around that when we were due to start tomorrow we would be entering virgin jungle away from all civilisation, and it would not be possible to fall out as no help could be given. Everyone was advised to carry only necessities. Most of the troops were now only carrying the bare necessities having already discarded or sold some of their kit to buy food.

Our rest came to an end all too soon. The following morning at first light found us again outside the camp lining up on the dusty road. We took our last look at the camp and wished we were still in there and set off. In less than one hour we passed alongside some paddy fields, and into the jungle. Almost immediately we were in muddy undergrowth, the air was damp and oxygen sapping, soon we were saturated in sweat, it was almost as bad as being under the blazing sun. It was impossible to know if everyone was keeping up as the terrain made it difficult for everyone to keep together. Our biggest problem would be to conserve the supply of water. We had all started out with water bottles full. I again resisted even attempting to take the stopper off my bottle till after at least three hours, even then I did not drink. I had to be very careful because in no way would I be able to replenish its contents until we reached the next camp. We did pass the odd stream and some risked having a drink it was impossible to stop them, as stated previously, having a drink is like a drug, once you start you can't stop and it's far worse in the tropical heat, when the sweat is pouring from you. We eventually stopped to eat our ration of rice and stinking dried fish, this fish seemed to be sun dried and uncooked, but it was better than nothing and helped the rice down. Dried fish turned out to be the standard for all meals taken out. Four o'clock arrived and I don't think we have travelled as far as the previous days, and it did not seem so difficult, probably because the going was slower. Suddenly we came into a clearing with a few native huts

news reaching us and it would not be possible to find out if anyone had been fortunate or able to carry a radio with them. It would also have been extremely risky and very dangerous if caught. We were regularly searched and it would happen at any time. A radio would have to be kept secretly buried and only brought out for a short while and in secret away from anyone, even our own men. We also worried about the food situation in the jungle. The only means of communication appeared to be by the river. At that time due to the monsoon it was very deep, wide and fast flowing. The boats we had seen on the river did not seem to have very powerful engines.

The boats into which we were crammed had flat bottoms, something like our barges at home but not so solid. The journey was up stream and in the fast flowing river the boats speed was very slow, at times we did not appear to make much head way and the heavy load of men did not help. The relaxing situation allowed us, for once, to enjoy the lovely scenery. Some times we passed through deep gorges with rocky cliffs covered in colourful vegetation. the screeching of all sorts of birds could be heard, occasionally monkeys could be seen at the waters edge or on large rocks helping themselves to a drink. Believe it or not, it was not uncommon to see a large fish rise from the water to try and take any small monkey on a rock, but usually the monkeys were too quick for them.

It was well after dark when our boat eventually drew to the side of the river, we scrambled over the side onto a steep bank into which had been hewed some rough steps. the bank rose to about thirty feet from the river to a short level piece of ground on which an atap roof structure had been built. We found this to be the cookhouse, a further climb up another bank and we were into our camp. Two huts had been completed and others were in the process of construction. There were some better quality huts several yards away, these probably housed the Japanese engineers who were going to be our taskmasters. We also found that other troops had arrived before us and had prepared a meal which turned out to be very poor, the Nips however, promised it would get better when boats would be organised to bring food up river, as this was the only means of getting food to us.

The Bangkok - Moulmein railway
sometimes known as
The Railway of Death

*Please note - the place named as KINSAYOK on this map
is referred to as KINSAYO throughout the book as this was
how it was generally known by us*

Chapter VII

Speedo, Speedo
On The Railway Of Death

The dawn of a new day arrived. It was now early November 1942. Nearly three weeks had passed since we left Singapore. The stifling journey by train and the agonising tramp through the jungle had taken its toll, every one was in a very weak state, some with dysentery, others with very sore feet. At least half of the men would not be fit enough to work and here we were, expected to build a railway through the jungle, which several construction companies from various countries had refused to take up the challenge because of the fear of the inevitable loss of life the work entailed.

The Nips however, demanded that all men who could get on their feet must work and the MO could not persuade them otherwise. Based on state of fitness the POWs were split into a number of parties. The fittest group had to walk a short distance and start to cut down mostly bamboo, this was the main type of vegetation growing close to the camp. The Nips had decided that a road back to Tarso was top priority. (An alternative route to the river.) Another group was detailed to dig latrines, this work involved digging a deep trench about three feet wide and fifty feet long, over which went several short lengths of bamboo lashed together with rattan tie to form a platform across the trench for the users feet. The distance between each platform would be about eighteen inches. The user would stoop over this space to do whatever into the trench. (Rattan tie is derived from the inside of bark from a certain tree it can be pulled off in long strips soaked in water to make it more pliable it is then used like very strong string it was very good and could be used in all sorts of situations.) Over these trenches a bamboo structure was erected each side of the trench and covered up to about four feet, then an open space to the roof which sloped to the rear from about seven feet. All of which was covered with atap.

The other group carried on building more huts, these were the standard type like others we had used, About one hundred metres long with a platform each side on which we slept, sat or whatever. An opening at each end acted as an entrance, with the usual atap covered sides and roof.

I found myself on the road party and with axes, shovels and crosscut saws we started to hack down the bamboo to make a clearing about twenty feet wide going in a southerly direction. The Nips had knocked in wooden posts to indicate width and direction of the road. No rests were allowed and we had to carry on without a break until the Nips shouted "All men Yasumi" for the lunch break which usually lasted about forty-five minutes. It was then back to work until evening when we returned to camp.

We found the camp had no enclosure and we were free to roam wherever we wished, no guards had been posted. The evening meal of rice and vegetables is taken soon after our return to camp, but first we had time to go to the river for a swim and clean up. This practice became routine at Kinsayo. The fact that no fencing was used or guards was obvious, In this jungle miles from any civilisation escape would be almost impossible. We found a small stream and waterfall close to the camp and risked taking water from it to drink. It was a very pleasant place to spend some time as we could sit and watch the various birds and listen to their song. At night we would make a camp fire outside our hut, make a drink if we had the makings or cook something to eat. This was the usual way evenings were spent. In this part of the world darkness came quite early.

The Nips had always kept a check on the number of POWs by counting us morning before work and at night after evening meal. They started the counting in Havelock Rd Singapore. The occupants of each hut lined up outside in rows, with the front row doing the counting. At first we numbered in English and the Nips somehow converted the numbers to their own. The first few times we numbered someone decided to say Jack then the next said Queen the next King instead of eleven twelve and thirteen, we could not help but snigger to one another. It was some time before one clever Nip twigged it, afterwards we had to number in Japanese. So if you could not count in Japanese you kept off the front row. We all very quickly learned to count in Japanese.

During the days that followed, several more batches of POWs arrived to fill the huts being built. One of which was used for the sick, but it was already full. The number of men falling sick increased daily, mainly due to the strenuous journey getting here. Malaria was starting to affect some of the troops. After all there was no anti malaria precautions and most of us have discarded mosquito nets. They buzzed around our bodies all night long. I can say that in Singapore and the whole of Malaya the mosquito was under control and Malaria was virtually non existent. The bamboo platform on which we sleep is riddled with bugs which crawled over our naked bodies in the night, they do not like daylight. They are about half the size of our Lady cow, the same shape and very dark red in colour, you can feel them crawling over your body and automatically squash them, the stink of ammonia is very strong. We are now also troubled with lice crawling over us. As we are in no position to apply very hot water to our clothing, now worn constantly, as most of us only have what we stand up in. Their eggs can be found in all the seams of clothing and no matter how we try it's impossible to squash all of them.

Since arriving at the camp and wandering around the jungle, we found a small "Kampong" quite close about half a mile away. I do not know where we got the name from, but a Kampong consists of a small cluster of native huts. The occupants seem very poor and probably live on fish from the river and chickens, which they have been selling to the troops. They are probably making more money a week now than they made in a whole year previously. The fishing lines outside a hut attracted my attention, and I decided to try and buy a line and some hooks. Approaching the Thai, I tried to make him understand what I wanted, but he laughed and said "Mi-me," which I eventually found out meant 'no,' but he also made me understand that when the next boat came up the river he would be able sell me a line and hooks. Visions of fish suppers flashed through my mind. The chickens have to be paid for and I have little money. The fish would be free, if I could get a bit of rice for the hook.

Since we started work with the Nips, they seemed to be quite ignorant of any modern method of doing things. We had to work with any sort of old equipment, the only tool for digging was called a chunkle. It had a straight handle about four feet long to which a piece of ten inch by six inch flat steel was attached at right angle to the shaft and the ground was dug with a chopping motion. Someone had a short rule and from that they cut lengths of bamboo one metre long and cut a notch in them at a quarter, half and three quarter point. These were the only ruler they used to build the railway. The work we did was very tiring in our weak state, the Nips had started to try and make us work faster, it was now "Speedo, speedo" all day long as the constant energy sapping sun blazed down on us. What a relief it was to get back to camp and rush to the river to get a dip in that lovely cooling water.

We had an added menace, Malaria, everyone had been affected, even myself. First you start to shiver, the body starts to shake vigorously, although the temperature is around the 100's you feel frozen so the only thing you could do was get under your blanket and let it have its fling. After about two hours the body seemed to change, you got warmer and warmer and soon you would start to sweat, but you had to stick it out and stay under your blanket, to try and cool down would have been disastrous, this condition carried on for about a day after which you were left considerably weaker as a result of the attack. It may surprise you to know that during the 'speedo' on the railway I was made to carry on working whilst having an attack of Malaria on several occasions. The Nips were so callous they demanded a specific number of men for each working party. Those men that were very weak could not stand it and died on the working party and were buried on the spot. The medical officer, although he tried his best was powerless trying to appeal to the Nips that certain men were not in a fit condition to go out to work, but it made no difference we had to go. Quite often a man would not make it to the place of work.

The Nips also had another brain wave to get sick men off their bed space. The latrines with the intense heat of the day began to stink to high heaven, consequently the area was covered in thousands of big black blue bottle flies, there were also a few of the small house type flies in our huts. The Nips told the MO that all men able to get off their bed space must catch 50 flies every day. These would be checked every evening at 'tenco.' (The evening count of POWs.) Well what did these sick men do! They walked or struggled to the latrine and within a few minutes got all the flies they needed. The Nips could not complain, they asked for flies and the men got them but in the easiest and quickest way possible. As stated previously there was no privacy going to the latrine, as many as twenty to thirty men could be using it at the same time. We would stoop down over the trench straddling bamboo about a foot from the next man. If that man happened to be a Eurasian Dutch man, (we had about three thousand of these Dutch troops working with us in this camp) you got a bath in the process. All paper had long since been used up so in the jungle we resorted to using the leaves from the trees. The Dutch however, always carried a bottle of water with them and after doing what they had to do splashed the water over themselves and whoever was next to them got caught in the slip stream.

The fact that we had several different nationalities living and working with us in the camp, meant cleanliness was very difficult to organise; the result was that dysentery was rife, hence the fly killing scheme. These problems together with the lack of food all combined to hasten the onset of acute sickness and in many instances ultimate early death. The situation was aggravated by the fact that we were in the jungle without the necessary medical supplies to combat those conditions. The Nips made no effort to help the situation. Soon after the Dutch arrived in Kinsayo, dysentery became rife, this situation with Malaria, Beri Beri, (a condition caused by malnutrition in which the body legs and feet swelled up enormously), and blindness, was taking toll of our lives at that time. The death toll mounted daily.

I eventually got my line and a couple of hooks from the Thai in the Kampong and looked forward to some evenings by the river. There was, however, a problem, I needed bait for the hook. It would mean forfeiting some of my meal of rice, but I would not be too happy about that. It would be no use going to the cookhouse as all food cooked was used up at each meal time. But I had a brain wave, I decided to go to the Nips, bow and beg for some of their left overs, and try to indicate to them what I wanted it for. They had a bit of a laugh to themselves, probably thinking I was mad, but gave me some rice. Returning to my hut I pummelled the rice in my mess tin with my spoon till I eventually got it to a nice smooth paste and hoped it would stay on my hook till I got a bite and went down to the river with my mate, it was nearly dusk, I had already got a length of thin bamboo from the jungle and managed to tie the line to the end. I had no such thing as a float, I just hoped that I would feel the fish when it took the bait. The hook was quite big and needed a lump of rice about one and a half inch in diameter. I thought a fish would have to be quite big to take it. We had been fishing for some time and it was getting quite dark but the moon had come up, the rice had nearly all gone, then I felt the rod leave my hand, I leaned forward and grabbed it in time, the line and most of the rod had been pulled into the river by something. I tried to lift the rod but couldn't make any headway, I then realised that there was a fish or something fighting me, I gradually pulled on the rod until I got to the line and bit by bit pulled on the line until something came to the surface in the moonlight I could just about see that it was a fish but what a whopper, I asked my mate to find a piece of wood and as I drew it to the side told him to give it a couple of blows on the head. He did and as we struggled to get it on the bank I dropped on top of it to stop it sliding back into the water. I suddenly realised the fish was about five feet long, we looked around and found a piece of rattan tie that we use when building the huts I hooked some tie round the gills slung it over my shoulder and set off up the bank towards our hut. The fishes head was by my shoulder its tail dragging on the ground. As we passed the cook house one of the cooks was still there and came to have a look and asked what I intended to do with it, until then I had not considered it any problem, to me it was just food. After some discussion I agreed to let him keep it in the cookhouse for safety overnight and suggested if he gutted and cooked it, for breakfast he could have a piece, the rest was shared with nearly thirty men who slept near me in our hut. That morning we had a piece of fish instead of our usual rice and brown sugar. It was much appreciated by all and they said I should do the same thing every night. We could not understand why the nips did not exploit the fact that the river was full of fish, with some explosive sufficient fish could be caught to provide a regular meal of fresh food, but we had noticed and experienced that they seemed rather slow to realise the obvious things.

The work in the jungle was now taking toll of our clothing, most of us for some time, only had what we stood up in. I was one of those people and the constant sweating with nothing to change into, the shirt and shorts had become very ragged, my boot tops had almost parted from the soles and would not last much longer. Some men were already in bare feet. When we stood in line ready to march off to work we looked a ragged lot and impossible to recognise from the smart British troops of nearly twelve months ago. Every Thursday we were given the day off and took the opportunity to try and do some repairs. It seemed that because, and only because the Nips wanted a days rest, we were given one too.

The days seem to pass very quickly, the work is terribly hard in the energy sapping jungle. We had to get up before dawn and outside for roll call. It's a farce, there is not a cat in hells chance of trying to escape. We were at least three hundred miles from friendly fire, the Thai's would give us away as there was a price on our heads. We would either die in the jungle or get shot on recapture for sure. The food had still not improved, in fact it had got worse. For breakfast it was a half pint of rice and a drink of hot river water. After which we would be given another half pint of rice and a piece of dried fish to take out for mid day on the working party. We would return to camp just before dusk worn out. After a quick bathe in the river we would have another half pint of rice and some veg, usually marrow, horrible, I don't know how we managed on it, but of course we didn't. It soon became dark, but there were no lights in the huts so we would sit outside talking mostly about food and any rumours about the war etc. If we had managed to catch anything in the jungle we would make a fire to cook and eat it. I remember whilst out on a working party one day I saw a snake sitting on a low branch, part of his body was quite swollen, so he was obviously lying there to digest whatever it had eaten. Quickly with both hands grabbing it by the tail I swung its head against the tree trunk to kill it. That night cutting it up to cook it we found a large rat inside the body, but that did not stop us from eating it, the flesh what little there was tasted a bit like pork and the skin like pork crackling. We went to bed that night a little more contented.

The sick in the hospital hut had no chance of getting any extra food and were dying rapidly it was just impossible to live on the rations supplied, so they were getting weaker and weaker. We had become used to burying the dead on a daily basis. They were just put into a rice sack and buried outside the camp, very close together. Someone did have a bugle so at least the last post could be sounded. The bugler was kept very busy.

December 1942 arrived and we had been issued with a printed post card to send home. Our officers advised us to give only good news to ensure getting them past the Jap. censors. At least our families would have some news from us. A scanned copy of both sides of the actual card I sent home to my parents is shown within. In fact I still have all the letters and cards I sent, all those years ago, after leaving England to go to war.

I never found out how long it took to get those cards sent and delivered to my parents, but in those days in the prison camps we often discussed whether or not our parents had been advised of our whereabouts. According to records official confirmation was received from the WarOffice on the 3rd of June 1943, stating that I was stationed in Malaya when Singapore fell, and that I was a prisoner of war. What agony my parents and family must have gone through, not knowing where I was, or whether I was alive or dead for seventeen months.

Our first Christmas as P.O.W's as far as food was concerned was no different than any other day. We had been promised Red Cross food parcels, but did not believe the Nips would let them through. It was true they never arrived. But surprise, surprise, although they do not celebrate Christmas, they gave us a day off. The officers arranged a concert, which took place on a spare piece of ground that had been cleared to build huts, there was no stage and no props, but what did it matter as long as we enjoyed it. With so many troops in the camp there was no shortage of talent. I remember the man who "brought the house down" as you might say. His mime of eating a bag of fish and chips out of a newspaper was hilarious. Even some of the Nips had gathered at the rear to watch, at first a few came, but with so much laughter going on it was not long before most of them came to stand around and watch. Obviously, being isolated in the jungle they also must have been very bored. The concert was a great success, and went on after the sun had

Front of card sent from POW camp.

From:
Name W.R. YATES
Nationality ENGLISH
Rank PTE.
Camp No. 6
    THAILAND

PASSED
P.W. 436

To:
MR. + MRS YATES
    252, SANDON RD. STAFFORD
  STAFFS, ENGLAND

(back of same card.)

IMPERIAL JAPANESE ARMY

Date 23·12·1942

Your mails (and ~~~~~~~~) are received with thanks.
My health is (good, ~~usual~~, ~~poor~~).
~~I am ill in hospital.~~
I am working for pay (~~I am paid monthly salary~~).
~~I am not working.~~
My best regards to ALL AT HOME. LES AND EMILY
AND RELATIVES.

Yours ever,

Roy

set. We built two large fires one on each side of where the acts took place and when the moon came up they were lit with the beautiful tropical light of a full moon. The silvery light was quite bright, this together with the fires enhanced the players doing their acts, it was far better than any stage lighting.

The work soon became more trying and the day off quickly forgotten. The Nips started to get irritable as less and less men became available for work. The hut being used for the sick was now constantly full, malnutrition, dysentery, beri beri and then tropical ulcers began to take their toll. A tropical ulcer develops from a bamboo scratch and soon spreads into a large open wound filled with puss, again with little or no medical supplies these soon spread over the leg into large open wounds and if not covered become fly blown and filled with maggots. The stench from the ulcer was terrible. It was common to see men sitting on their bed space with the wound covered, then to quickly remove the pad and try to pluck off the maggots before they burrowed out of view. In some way they did useful job by eating away the puss but the down side was they also ate the good flesh. Medical orderlies would try to swab away the puss daily but as they could only apply a saline dressing the ulcers in some cases spread over the whole leg with the result that it had to be amputated. I did hear that in some camps this operation was done without anaesthetic.

The nips would go into the sick hut each morning to try and find men to go out to work anyone who could get off their bed space was ordered out to join the working party. So the men with ulcers sat on the edge of their bed space with their ulcers uncovered. The stench soon drove the Nips out of the hut, after which they did not go in again. We very often found them to be extremely scared of any infection. By this time I had experienced several bouts of malaria which took me out of action for two days.

Whilst at Kinsayo I spent many evenings fishing the river and was very successful in providing myself and several mates with evening meals. Not only was I getting extra food the time spent by the river was very relaxing. I remember one night in particular, sitting peacefully watching the monkeys playing on the rocks on the other side, which was a good fifty yards away, (the river was very wide at Kinsayo). Suddenly I felt a pulling motion on the line, but then nothing else happened, it seemed as though the line was caught up on the river bed, then the line moved and I realised that something had taken my bait, taking the strain on the line I tried to raise what I assumed to be a fish to the surface I got it so far then whatever it was pulled the line back towards the riverbed. This up and down motion carried on for several minutes, eventually I managed to overcome my catch and get it to surface near the side of the river. I then got the shock of my life, it was a turtle I had caught. My mate who was with me helped me to lift it out of the water and on to the bank, before I had time to remove the hook it started to walk back towards the river, we brought it back and I removed the hook, as I did this it looked straight at me with its sad eyes and my brain said let it go free, but my stomach was hungry and said no way. We carried it back to a patch outside our hut to decide what to do with it. I tied one of its legs with a piece of rattan to one of the bamboo supports of our hut and sat down on the ground to decide what to do. It was food and had to be killed, but even though I was hungry I could not do it, some one said cut its head off. Well the turtle was about two feet six inches in diameter and no one had a knife big enough to do the job with one thrust, so we decided to go and find one of the cooks. Our luck was in, the one we spoke to had been a butcher and had no pangs at doing the job, he brought with him one of the large knives from the cookhouse and with one stroke severed its head, but to our amazement it still walked around. We then proceeded to remove its shell with the knife and it still moved. We took the flesh to the small river not far from the camp to wash and cut it to smaller pieces to go in the pot which was already waiting to cook it, as it was being cut into smaller pieces they still quivered, it was most strange. It was an episode in my life which I will never forget. Those turtles eyes remain vivid in my memory to the present day. The turtle shell became my seat outside the hut when we built our fire in the moonlight at the end of a very hard days work.

The camp was becoming very big as several thousand native Dutch troops had been arriving. They were not very clean in their habits and consequently more dysentery was breaking out. We tried to keep as far away from them as possible but we all had to use the same latrines.

Whilst at Kinsayo I remember one evening in particular, I had returned back to camp after a hard days work in the jungle and as usual went for a wash and swim, I was relaxing and enjoying the coolness of the water, when the sound of a boats engine reached my ears, I turned to swim towards the bank to ensure my safety. The boat, several minutes later rounded the bend in the river and steered towards the bank were I was sitting. Several Nips from the camp came running down to the river side, they were in a boisterous giggling mood and began to unload food and other boxes from the boat, I then noticed some Japanese women being helped ashore there were about ten of them. They all made their way to the huts occupied by the Japs. Being nosy I followed but returned to my own hut to pass on the news of what I had seen. A short while later some one came into the hut to say that a screen had been erected outside in an open space close to their cookhouse, we all raced out to find that the Nips had planned to show a film and that we would be welcome to stand and watch it. Although it was in Japanese we found no difficulty in following the plot, it was the usual boy meets girl stuff but what surprised me was that although the boy loved the girl, there was an element of corporal punishment. When for no reason the boy gave his girl a viscous slap across the face.

We eventually found out that the girls I saw had come to give them a good time, they were Geisha Girls. We had a bit of a laugh about it and of course being men it was discussed if given the opportunity would they. The result without doubt was that in their present weak state women were furthest from their thoughts.

With the arrival of the Dutch the POW camp was now full and all the huts occupied. In the last few days we had finished cutting a path through the jungle for a considerable distance in both directions. Several Elephants had been used to clear the large trees, some of which being tall and straight had been collected together for future use. The rest of the work had been done with our bare hands and shoulders, each day we would return to camp exhausted with aching bodies and sore shoulders, the intense heat and constant attack by insects sapped what little energy we had. Had I not experienced it, I would not have believed the body could have stood up to so much torture. But of course in many instances it didn't. The Railway Of Death Was Beginning To Take Its Toll.

It was a regulation in the Japanese army to have the hair shaved off the head and so an instruction was given that all POWs must have their hair shaved off, they said it was more hygienic. Now most of us had already used up all the razor blades we had and therefore stopped shaving, so the only POWs without beards were those with cut throats or Rolls razors. What a sight we looked, with no hair on our heads and a beard and in either ragged khaki drill, or just a pair of ragged shorts. In the heat it was an advantage having no hair, but I personally found myself with a sore chest with the constant rubbing of the sweaty beard. What a sight I must have looked, but that was furthest from my thoughts.

As previously stated we were getting paid to work, a pittance of twenty-five cents a day, duck eggs were ten cents each, and most of us would buy several a week. I think that the Thai, duck egg was responsible in saving thousands of POW lives during our time as prisoners, thankfully they were in plentiful supply. The Nips discouraged us from buying from the Thai's, but even they realised that to get the maximum out of us, tended to not be too bothered about us buying food. Someone would be organised to sit by the river to watch out for the food boats coming up river, once the signal was given it was a mad rush to get there, mostly we would buy eggs, goola malaka sugar, and tobacco to make cigarettes. The goola malaka was a soft brown sugar and very useful to have, specially at breakfast time as all we got for breakfast was a half a pint of rice.

I would like you to imagine what our life was like in the POW camps in the jungle, how long would you last if you had to live in constant hunger and exhaustion, at the same time work in the jungle from shortly after dawn till dusk. Just try this for one day wake up at six am, cook yourself a porridge of soggy rice that would just fill a teacup, (you will have to imagine the fact that our rice had weevils and the occasional piece of mouse muck), if you were lucky enough to have bought some sugar add say one teaspoonful and a small cup of warm water. Then picture having to walk several miles into a jungle and work till about midday. Have another cup of rice, but this time it would be cold cooked dry rice, (as you would have in a curry) with a small piece of dried stinking fish and a drink of water. Then back to work, just think, the temperature is well over 100 degrees, your body is unprotected, the sweating and energy sapping work is killing, you may also suffer a beating by one of your guards, it happened every day. At dusk totally exhausted you stagger back to camp, another two or three miles, then you can enjoy your evening meal, another cup of dry rice but this time you boil a small amount of greens and pour it over the rice together with the water the greens were boiled in. For a drink, it's another cup of warm water. So how do you feel at the end of the day, how long do you think you would last. Slowly the body is starved until it is too weak to fight, disease and depression sets in. Death when it comes is almost a relief. Also remember that the railway took over twelve months to build and took the lives of twenty thousand of my fellow POWs out of a total of sixty thousand. The total death toll on the railway including natives amounted to in the region of over one hundred thousand. So how did I and those others who survived and lived through this terrible ordeal and suffering come through? It can be explained in just a few words. A visualisation, with

God's help that one day you would go home, together with an unwavering Will Power to survive no matter what you had to face.

Having cut a channel through the jungle many metres wide for quite a distance, the next stage of our work began. The Japanese engineers had driven in a double line of pegs to indicate the path of the railway embankment, which we then had to build each day on arrival at the site with wicker baskets and chunkles, (Chinese spades.) The baskets were to be used to carry the earth dug out with the chunkles to form the embankment. These baskets were made of wicker, about two feet in diameter and a foot deep with two wicker handles. We had to work in groups of three, one digging and two carrying. The Nip would mark out a piece of ground three metres square. Our daily task required us to dig out and carry the equivalent of a cubic metre of earth for every man in your group. You will have to imagine what an arduous daily task this was. This did not mean that the Japanese had brought in mechanical excavators, no our hands and small tools were to be the excavators. To dig down to a depth of one metre over three square metres and carry all the loose earth by hand to dump it and form a mound twenty metres away in a tropical temperature of about one hundred and twenty degrees meant that it would be an almost impossible task for some of the weaker men in the groups. But it had to be done before we could return to camp. There was no time for a rest, it involved hundreds of journeys backwards and forwards with your basket of earth. It seemed that once it was loosened with the chunkle there was three times the amount to carry away. In our weak state, sweat poured off every one, running into our eyes and dripping on to the ground, the task always took a full day to complete, the Nips would come and measure the finished hole there were no allowances, any unfinished holes had to be completed by others helping out, we would then be allowed to return to camp. This work proved to be one of the most difficult and energy sapping tasks on that hellish railway. The Korean guards were always present to help out, by giving us a belt across the back with a piece of bamboo to make us work harder. These barbaric actions were done to impress the Japanese engineers, who I am afraid were just as bad. If the bamboo had split it would cause nasty open cuts across the body, with often disastrous results, due to lack of medical supplies and the very weak state of the body.

Other degrading incidents happened when all our huts and kit was searched. It was done quite regularly by the I.J.A. military police. We would be turned out and the Jap police used Korean guards to assist them.

Two of our own officers were allowed to be present, all personal belongings would be tipped out, the whole hut would be virtually turned over and the personal belongings would be mixed up. They would take knives and anything they were not sure of. In those days the Japs seemed very uncivilised and backward compared with the present generation. I remember quite clearly, they would copy anything produced in the western world as it was always better than theirs. They firmly believed and in fact told me personally that we had to put two engines in our planes to make them go as fast as theirs with only one engine. Their ignorance was amazing, many articles normally used by Europeans they had never seen, and would do anything to secure fountain pens, wristwatches, petrol lighters. Any one who was lucky enough to possess a Rolls razor had to secretly hide it, they were so valuable. However, most of us had sold anything of value to buy food.

In the Japanese army the NCOs are very powerful compared with our ranks. For instance a gunso is equal to our sergeant and he is allowed to carry a sword, they looked very funny really, being so small the sword often dragged along the ground as they walked. The gunso most often was the camp commander. A corporal was called a hancho and also had quite a lot of power, he was very often seen punishing their own other ranks.

The standard practice of mild punishment in the Japanese Army involved the offender being made to stand to attention in front of the NCO who then struck the offender several vicious blows across the face with the flat hand or fist. We POWs also regularly received this same punishment at the slightest provocation. Having already personally suffered this treatment on several occasions, I can assure readers that it is very painful and humiliating, particularly when you realise we had to stand and take the punishment from a little insignificant five foot man standing in front of you. We all felt that the Japanese at that time were to a degree, still somewhat uncivilised. The reason being, we knew when to expect a beating because we would see the look in their eyes change dramatically to a wild hatred stare. So to sum up the various methods of punishment we had to suffer. Struck across the face with flat hand or fist, beaten with bamboo that could leave open wounds and there was no medication to help them heal, so gangrene often set in. After punishment we could also have been made to stand in the tropical sun all day, shot or beheaded. There were many other types of punishment talked about, but I only intend to mention those which I was aware of. I did not see or hear of anyone confined to a sweat box for several days, as depicted in the film, "Bridge on the River Kwai." There were, however, undoubtedly many forms of punishment and torture.

Having actually started to build the railway and working on the embankment the Nips then started to make the officers work side by side with the troops and were often found more arduous tasks. Everybody even the sick now had to get up before dawn and struggle around in the dark, or some had the luxury of a flickering coconut oil lamp to see with, actually an empty milk tin with a hole in the lid and a few strands of string for a wick. Breakfast was issued soon after daybreak and at 7.30am it's roll call, every one except those that cannot get up off their bed must attend. The guards then check the numbers and select some of the sick who they think are capable of work, some they picked were really too ill. But no matter how much the M.O. protested the sick ones were marched off to join the ranks of the fit working party. Working tools are then handed out and the whole party is marched off to walk the mile or two, to begin a day of misery under the relentless tropical sun. Very often one or two of the very sick who should never have been forced to work would not return and were buried in the jungle, not far from where they worked. At about 6.30pm or when everyone had completed their task with blistered hands and swollen feet, we drag and stumble our tired and aching bodies back to camp. The surprising part of the conditions under which the troops were living and working seemed to bring out the best in everyone. Although we all came from different Regiments, the comradeship was magnificent. Every one had to look after themselves, but the policy of "Damn you Jack, I'm all right" had gone. There was a feeling of, we are all in this together and if you could help someone in a worse state, who needed a hand, you helped without hesitation. I saw men carrying other men's tools back from the working party, it was not a strange sight to see men being carried back to camp by the fittest. In one camp in particular I personally had the experience, when very ill and weak, of being carried to and from the latrines by a friend for several days.

Day after day without respite the work on the embankment and other associated jobs went on. The death roll mounting as the days passed. The piece of ground just outside the camp used as a burial ground gradually had to be extended. The existence was a misery, no news from the outside world only rumours. After a strenuous day in the jungle, a swim in the river to ease our aching bodies, the evening meal, if you could call it that, would be eaten. It would then be dark and we would enjoy the best part of the day.

Wood brought in from the jungle would be used to light fires outside the huts, any one lucky enough to have been able to get anything from the jungle, would cook and eat it. Most of us would just sit around the fire, talk about home, how long the war would last, discuss any rumours that were being passed around, the topic of food predominated and we would visualise enjoying a good meal. Under normal conditions a tropical evening, sitting round a camp fire would be magical. The cloudless sky with a full moon, creates a beautiful silvery glow to trees, vegetation and buildings. The air is filled with the sounds of nocturnal creatures and because of the stillness of the night seemed to be louder than the sounds experienced during the day. Eventually we would retire for the night, enter our hut and drop onto our allotted two and a half feet of bed space, pull our blanket over us and go to sleep, only to be disturbed by attacking mosquitoes and squashing vile ammonia smelling bugs as they crawled across your chest. The split bamboo on which we slept was full of them. Occasionally during the day we would untie the bamboo and take it outside in the sun and strike the ground with it to remove the bugs. It was fun to watch them scamper off, but only for a few feet, as the strong sunlight killed them very quickly.

The date was now April 1943, I had already experienced several bouts of Malaria by this time. It generally strikes without warning, I personally experienced one bout whilst out on a working party, The attack started in the middle of the morning, I was so wracked with the shakes a Nip for once took pity on me and told me to lie down in the shade. He would not let me go back to camp and I had to have some help to get me back to my hut at the end of the days work. I was allowed one days rest on the following day, after which it was back to work. Once the attacks of malaria started I began to have re-occurring bouts regularly every few weeks. By now, due to a lack of medical supplies, insufficient food, no rest, we were getting weaker and weaker. The number of men completely unable to work and gradually losing interest in life and looking like skeletons mounted daily. A couple of huts had been built and used as a hospital. Walking in to see someone you knew was terribly distressing. There would be bodies swollen with Beri Beri, some hidden under their blanket waiting to die. Some with enormous holes in their legs with not enough bandage to cover the stinking gangrene tropical ulcer that was spreading and getting bigger each day. The only treatment being saline, (salt water swab). I remember one poor man in particular, the ulcer had spread and was so big, it was decided that the only way to save him meant amputation. It was done without anaesthetic, several men held him down until the pain drove him unconscious. The ulcers usually developed initially from a bamboo scratch, the body being in such a week state could not fight the poison inflicted by the bamboo. Other men had Dengue Fever and sat there with shrivelled bodies and deeply sunken staring eyes. The sight of these men can only be described as unbelievable, particularly when one considers and realises that not many months ago they were fully fit, strong and fearless soldiers in the British Army. At that time over twenty-five per cent of the men in that camp, were extremely sick and in all probability facing certain death. They had reached a stage of the hopeless realisation of their condition and the ongoing situation we were all in, the body and mind had given up that it would ever end, and had thus decided, 'this is it, lets get it over with.' As the numbers of the chronically sick continued to rise the Nips eventually realised that these men would be of no further use to them and it was decided to send them down river to the base camp at Kanchanburi where they would receive better food and medical supplies. I was later to find that the camp at Kanchanburi was quite good compared with our conditions in the jungle. The food was much better, and some medical supplies were available. In fact some of the men picked up and got stronger, but probably not enough to work again.

Reading this you may be wondering why I survived and had the strength and will to struggle on and manage to work on this infamous railway to its completion, outlive all the misery and torture our captors inflicted, and suffer the hunger and eventual death it may have entailed. In principal there were two main reasons. Firstly, an indomitable steadfast will power to survive no matter what, whilst having a vision that one day I would be free to go home. Every single British soldier, taken prisoner in Singapore, who could not, or did not have this power and vision perished in their hell camps. My second reason concerned food. In order to be able to work and survive my body needed extra food over and above the meagre ration supplied by the Japanese. We could buy the few eggs and a little sugar with our twenty-five cents pay, but this was by no means sufficient to sustain the body. The rest of the food which I needed came from snakes, fish and another very dangerous source, a Japanese food store over which two Japanese slept. This food had to be stolen and I became involved in a very strange way. When we first arrived in the jungle camp and settled in the hut, I began to notice a man whose bed space was on the other side from where I slept. He always had something to eat and a smoke. One day I strolled across the hut to have a chat with him, he offered me some of what he was eating and said he was in the East Surrey Regiment and lived in London, but I am not prepared to state his name for obvious reasons. Asking him where he obtained the food, he smiled but would not say.

I had my suspicions, there could only be one source, the Jap.stores. My mind and thoughts began to race with visions of some extra food, but dare I have a go, the risk if caught could be life threatening. Luck was with me, two days later I had to join several others engaged to unload stores from a wagon. I immediately realised that divine providence seemed to be leading me to take the risk and become a thief. Whilst on the party I surveyed the layout inside taking particular attention of how the door was fastened. There were just two loops of rattan tie through which a length of bamboo was placed to keep the door closed. I realised that it would be quite easy to put my hand through the rattan and feel for the bamboo and carefully slide the bamboo upwards to release it from the lower loop, then downwards to release it from the upper loop, then carefully lower it to the floor. The hut was divided into two parts. The front section consisted of several sets of shelving on which was stacked with tins of food, various types of vegetables, fruit of various sorts, tobacco and cigarettes, and other types of food I had never seen before. The front section was divided from the rear section by a partition with a three feet opening in the centre. The rear section contained two beds, obviously for the Japanese store men. I made a mental note of the complete layout without saying a word to the others on the party. That night I lay on my bed space thinking out a plan of action. I felt sure I could get in, I also realised that I should only take a small quantity in the hope it would not be missed. I would then be able to repeat the exercise. I also worked out how to replace the bamboo on exit. I also decided to take my haversack, (empty of course) which I hoped to fill with food and perhaps some cigs. With the plans made I dropped off to sleep.

The day that followed was one of the most worrying days of my life. For the whole of the day I kept going over my plans realising that if caught, without doubt I would be shot. But I kept trying to put it out of my mind, I was determined to take the chance that night. As usual I spent the evening sitting round our little camp fire and eventually went in my hut to lie down, but could not sleep. However, I must have eventually dropped off because I was awakened by someone near who had to go to the latrines. This was nothing out of the ordinary, in fact there was a regular procession to and from the 'lats' all night long. I slid off my bed space wearing just my loin cloth picked up my haversack and like the others made my way to the 'lats.' I hung around in there for a few minutes until all was clear then made a sprint down to the riverside. I took off my loin cloth and put it in my haversack, I was completely nude, I then smeared my body with the soft wet earth, till no white skin was left, looking up to the sky the moon had already disappeared and I had no idea what the time was. Tuning my ears for the least sound I made my way to the Japanese store hut and lay on the ground by the door for almost a minute listening for any sound, all was quiet and I raised myself onto my haunches and carefully put my left hand through the atap to feel for the bamboo rod. (I used my left hand because it is more dextrous than the right). With some surprise my hand was spot on and without the slightest sound moved it upwards until I felt it free from the lower loop, then slid it slowly down until the cane was free in my hand. I slid my right hand through the atap lower down and gently lowered the cane to the floor and carefully opened the door enough to let me in. I squatted on my haunches for a few seconds listening for any sounds, all was quiet and I stood up as my eyes had already adjusted to the darkness inside. I quickly selected what I wanted from the shelves almost filling my haversack. I surprised myself I had not made the slightest sound. Moving towards the door I picked up the cane, almost closing the door I placed the cane in its lower loop, put my left hand again through the atap grasped the cane closed the door and slid the cane up into the top loop. The door was shut and fastened. I quickly slunk away congratulating myself. My dexterity during the whole episode really surprised me. I was on a high. Realising that thieves not only stole to make money. It was also a thrilling experience. I made my way down to the river washed off and replacing my loin cloth sauntered back towards the latrine and then my hut. Outside the hut under the space where I slept I scraped a hole in the soft earth and put in the tins of food replaced the earth and made it look firm. The tobacco and other odd things would be kept in my haversack. There was enough room. Eventually I lay down to go to sleep. I was so full of hype, sleep eluded me that night. In all I had been away from my bed space for no more than an hour.

The following night after returning from the working party and settled on my bed space, I made a cig, with some tobacco and a dry leaf and also found something to eat. Looking over towards the man from the East Surrey's, he was staring at me in disbelief and was soon off his bed and came across to me and asked where the food had come from. I looked back at him smiling and said, "Probably the same place as you." He said nothing for a while and seemed rather surprised, eventually he said, "It's no good, you must not go in again, it will not work." He obviously did not want any one else encroaching on what he considered to be his territory. I replied,"If you can do it so can I, you cannot stop me." He did not say anything for a while and then told me he lived in London as a civilian before call up and was by profession a burglar. This did not surprise me, he looked the type. "I have a proposition" he said, "Let's join forces, I'll teach you all I know and we will go out together." The first thing he told me was that we would be going out on the job between three thirty and four thirty as at this time of the night people were in their deepest sleep. I am pleased to say without going into more detail, that our operations carried on without detection for the whole of the time we were together in several camps. Without doubt it was the second principal reason why I survived to tell this story. I can also say that on my return to civilian life, I did find it extremely difficult to resist the temptation to take something which registered on my mind as being easy to steal. However, in complete honesty I have managed to resist the temptation, but it's been very difficult.

Whilst on the subject regarding my return to civilian life from the prison camps, some fifty or more years ago it should be realised that in those days there was no such help by counselling after such a traumatic experience. We just had to get on with it and try to adjust to a normal way of living. I do know that after all the years that have passed some ex POWs still suffer from terrible nightmares. Luckily my nightmares stopped many years ago. They always followed the same pattern. Two Japanese soldiers would come to my house, order me out and march me to the railway station, to take me back to the prison camp.

After spending many weeks building the embankment, which was at that time well on its way. I found myself transferred to a bridge building party. At least it was something different to do. But we were also told that the bridge building would be at another camp further up river. This news was a little worrying as it entailed another march through the jungle and the monsoon season was about to begin. It had improved slightly at Kinsayo because the road had been completed to that camp and supplies of food were being brought up in motor vehicles with the occasional ration of a very small amount of fresh meat, if you were lucky enough to get some in your ration, at least it tasted better.

Several days later we were told to be ready to move off at day break the next morning. What a sight we all looked that morning when lining up to move off. The officers looked reasonably dressed in shorts and shirt with their haversacks on their backs. The men, some in ragged shorts but no shirt, some in just a loin cloth, (we called them 'Jap happies' because this was what the Japs wore when relaxing during their free hours in camp). Our haversack on our back carried most of our belongings to which we attached such things as groundsheet, blanket, mess tins, drinking receptacles made out of empty tins with a bit of wire for a handle. We also carried empty four gallon petrol cans with a wire handle which we kept under our bed spaces filled with water for a quick wash each morning. (Most of us had no soap though). Our boots had mostly worn out, so some men had cut off some of the uppers to show bear toes, others had made straps to fasten over the foot with just the sole left, others had made 'clop clops' with wood, some even bare foot. What a sight we all looked when setting off that morning, with the cans rattling against each other on our backs. Some men had used two bamboo poles, attached an empty rice sack and used it like a stretcher to carry their belongings, they walked one behind the other with the stretcher resting on their shoulders. Some even had small packs strapped on their chests. It should be realised that we had by then reached a stage in our lives as prisoners that we had to carry all our belongings whenever we moved to another camp. Fortunately, the distance we had to go was short, just over ten miles, which brought us to a camp called Rin Tin. There were several huts but all deserted, as the place was now disused. The river was close so we had time for a bathe. There was evidence of its former occupation as we noticed the graves of several hundred men. We had already heard rumours of the heavy death rate in this camp and the graves proved that the news had been true.

The next morning we were on the move again, this march was much harder over hilly and dense jungle, following a winding narrow track. The going was much more difficult, being up hill and down dale. The distance was about fourteen miles and it took us about ten hours. Our staying powers were very poor those days, we were tired out. The Nips had to give us long halts, to enable the party to be kept together. The worst trouble was the old enemy, lack of water. Being hilly country, there were no streams to supplement our meagre supply of water in our bottles. By about four in the afternoon the Nips allowed a long halt as everyone was completely exhausted. They seemed to have learned at last that it was impossible to flog us along, if they wanted to get any work out of us later. An hour later, thank God we heard the sound of running water, every one rushed in the direction of the sound and we came across a mountain stream. We all dropped our kit and fell to the ground and put our heads into the cool running water having a drink at the same time, it was heavenly. There was not the slightest thought that the water may have been contaminated, no one cared. There was no doubt that not far from this stream, there would be a native compound of a few huts positioned to use the stream as their source of water. We had all been warned many times that most even running water should be boiled before using it for a drink. Cholera could strike and the result would be fatal. Eventually we arrived at a camp called Hindato.

Hindato

Our huts had previously been built by others already in the camp who had been employed on the embankment. This was a Godsend as the following day the monsoon started. We had again been lucky to get the march over before it started. When it rains in Thailand, it rains. without a stop day after day. On the working party we were soon up to our knees in water and mud and constantly irritated by a cloud of midges buzzing around our heads, sheer agony all day long.

The embankment passing through Hindato was almost finished by the men already there. Our job was going to be a little more specialised, bridge building, the jungle in this area had several gullies, through which streams flowed. At these points the embankment came to an abrupt end. Our first job found us cutting down saplings to act as scaffold, also selecting straight trunked trees at least thirty feet tall and with a diameter of about fourteen to eighteen inches. The amazing thing about this work, the Nip engineers had no measuring equipment. From one rule one metre long they went into the jungle and cut bamboo canes to the length of their original, these were the only measures they used for the whole of our bridge building work. The saplings had to be bundled and brought to the area of operation, together with the tree trunks which we found were going to be used as piles. An elephant and Thai driver had been engaged to drag the saplings and trunks to the clearing. Soon we were engaged in erecting a scaffold by tying the saplings together with rattan tie. Sections of scaffold would be connected together on the ground and then hoisted up by man power with ropes and pulleys. The sections would then be connected together with cross pieces to make the scaffold stable. It was quite entertaining to watch the Nips climbing and swinging up aloft during erection. They were quite adept at it and seemed quite safe in their rubber boots. On the ground we were standing either in mud or water, the monsoon although cooling the temperature a little made life and work more difficult as some of the men started to get foot rot.

Once the scaffold had reached its required height, pulley wheels would be attached, to enable the tree trunk piles to be hoisted into position, the piles had a shallow hole drilled into the top, after hoisting, a long steel bar and two ton concrete weight with a hole through the centre and two eyes would be positioned, so that the weight would slide up and down the steel shaft directly onto the pile acting like a hammer to drive it into the ground. A single rope from each eye on the weight was attached to twenty individual guy ropes positioned outside the scaffold. Forty men, twenty each side would be used to raise the weight and then let it fall to strike the pile and thus drive it into the ground. The amazing part about this work, we found that working in unison, raising the weight it seemed to be weightless. The motion of driving in the pile was a continuous process. The Nips would sing a repeating phrase and encourage us to join in the singing of "Ichi nee no sayo no sayo," then release the weight. The sing song would equal three pulls on the weight, (ichi nee is one two in Japanese.) So in Japanese one to ten is "Ichi nee san see go roko shichi hachi koo jue," (spelt as pronounced,) so we knew what ichi nee stood for but I never understood what sayo meant. Sometimes the pile would go in about two metres quite easily and the Nips would be quite happy. Sometimes it would only be driven in less than two feet because of rock. Sometimes the pile split and had to be replaced. That situation made them loose their temper and some of us would receive a beating, because of the amount of time lost replacing them. The piles would be driven in line in sets of five and set about one metre apart. The tops would then be cut off level, at the same time a tenon would be formed to fit into the mortised cut out of the cross piece. These cross pieces were manufactured from thicker sections of tree trunk, chipped flat on two sides to sit squarely on the pile with their mortised cut outs. Once completed the structure would then be bridged to support the rail track. The bridges took on many forms and were built according to the terrain. One in particular stood many hundreds of feet above the ground and was keyed into and around the side of a hill. I personally was not involved on that one as it was some way down river, but I did hear that it had cost many lives to build, by men falling off whilst working on the structure. I remember the bridge quite well because when I eventually went down river on the train, it was quite frightening as when passing over, the structure seemed to feel rather unstable and looking out of the wagon was nothing but a deep ravine below.

One particular episode whilst working on the bridges will remain in my memory forever. Once the scaffold was erected my main task involved pulling on one of the forty guy ropes to raise and release the weight to drive in the pile, which was rather monotonous, as stated, forty men all pulling together, very little effort was needed and I naturally became bored and my eyes were attracted to the Elephant to my right struggling with a pile caught up against a tree stump. The Thai.driver was getting irritated and hacked at the animals head with his hooked driving stick causing blood to spurt out, they were often very cruel, the animal would experience considerable pain from the sharp pointed hook going into its head. As I watched, I suddenly felt something strike my back, the pain and shock sent me dizzy, I turned to see a Nip behind me with a bamboo stick, looking into his eyes I saw that wild barbaric uncivilised glare which we all knew so well and had at some time or other experienced the cruel punishment that followed. He swore at me in Nipon and in English saying "English soldier no good, dammy, dammy" with both hands on the stick he raised it to strike again, I turned my back on him to carry on pulling the guy rope, with all his power the next blow struck my back the pain was excruciating and travelled throughout my body like an electric shock, another blow quickly followed and my head began to spin. My brain raced with thoughts of how I could try to stop the pain and agony of my situation, should I drop to the ground in the hope that he would stop, my mind said no, do not cower to this insignificant little man remember you are a British Soldier. I braced my body and carried on pulling on the rope as the blows continued. I lost count as my senses began to leave me and my body became numb, my grip on the rope slackened and I felt my hands sliding down the rope, then I must have blacked out. I never did find out if he continued to thrash me, I was told that no one was allowed to help me for some time then eventually I was carried away from the bridge by two comrades and given a drink from my water bottle. I was allowed to rest and the same two comrades helped me back to camp at the end of the days work. My whole body ached but I still felt numb from the beating. Once back in camp I was taken to the hospital hut and seen by the Medical Officer, he was very surprised to find that my skin had not been broken, I am now sure that the hand of providence had again stepped in and protected me because any open wounds were susceptible to gangrene setting in due to a lack of medical supplies. The M.O. managed to keep me in the hospital hut for two days then it was back to work.

Typical bridge structure.

A recent picture of a bridge that still stands to this day.

On my return to join the bridge building party the Nips had put some-one else into my position on the pile driving work and I was ordered to work with the elephant. The Nip would take me into the jungle and show me the material to be brought into the bridge area that day. There would be tree trunks to be used as piles, and bundles of saplings for scaffold, as soon as the Elephant with his Thai. driver arrived they would follow me, the ani-mal would be dragging a length of chain attached to its harness. To pick up the pile or bundle the elephant was trained to raise the pile or bundle at one end to allow me to put a noose round it with the chain so that it would lock tight when being pulled along. The piles were no problem, but it was diffi-cult to arrive back at the bridge with a complete bundle of scaffold, quite often if the noose was not tight enough.

At the end of each day the Nip would check all that I had brought to the clearing that day, always there were items I had not collected, no way could I remember exactly where everything was, the jungle was so dense it was like a maze, the result was inevitable, each night I had to stand to attention while he gave me several vicious slaps across the face, the standard mild form of punishment. It was however, still very painful.

The Thai was very cruel to his animal, quite often he would loose his temper and strike it on the head viciously with his driving stick which had a sharp pointed steel hook on the end, the beast would bellow as blood squirted from the wound, in return the elephant would try to take it out of me by trying to lash me with its very short tail, usually across my face, the bristles on his tail were very wiry and sharp, not very pleasant, he would also take a step back on my foot with one of his rear legs, but as the ground was soft and moist it had no effect. My problems mounted when another elephant was brought in to help, he was joined by a baby elephant from whom I had no peace, he was very playful running about backwards and forwards, I had to keep my eyes on it constantly, if not he would come running at me catch me when bending sending me flying face down, he thought it was great fun. At night after work I would walk to a small stream in the jungle to get water and have a wash, the working elephants would be free to roam but have their two front feet hobbled, to prevent them travelling too far, if they were about and saw me they would raise their trunks bellow and chase me, I would have to run like mad back to camp to get out of their way. They did not seem to bother any one else, just me I suppose they thought I was the one making them work. It is said an elephant never forgets, it must be true.

The monsoon was still causing us considerable misery on the working party, the area around each bridge was like a sea of black mud, the men would be standing in it all day long. Some of the bridges spanned a gully with a small stream. Day after day the work went on until some weeks later we were told our job was finished and that we would be moving to another camp to build more bridges.

When we arrived at our new camp we found there were no huts, just a jungle clearing, the area was called Qui-ima, (spelt as it sounded.) Only a few miles from Hindato camp. To add to our misery we had to sleep in tents. Some were badly torn and let the rain in, but we only stayed for a few days after which we arrived at another camp not far away called Qui- ichi. Again there were no huts, just a jungle clearing beside the railway embankment. We had to erect seven tents, six for one hundred and twenty men and one for five officers, they were not complete tents, just fly sheets of Indian tents. The fly sheets were part of the standard Indian army tent which slept eight men, four each side. We had to sleep ten each side, packed in like sardines. I thanked God that the monsoon was now over as some of the tents were not water proof. We did manage to erect a low platform of bamboo each side of the tent to sleep on. The situation and living conditions were now worse than at any time since our captivity. The food ration had also deteriorated due to lack of supplies. We noticed many hundreds of natives passing by our camp daily, walking north on the railway embankment. Our Nip engineers told us that they had been engaged to work on the railway. The shortage of food and living conditions soon took its toll, numbers of men falling sick and dying increased daily, it was very depressing and for the first time I began to loose heart and went down with a severe attack of malaria, experiencing bouts regularly, instead of snapping out of it I became weaker and weaker, to the extent that I was too weak to walk to the latrine and had to be carried by my closest friend and mate; a friendship which had started from the day we met way back in Havelock Rd camp in Singapore. Several days went by and my weakness began to continue to deteriorate until one morning on wakening I sat up, (as stated twenty in the tent,) we slept that close together virtually touching one another, the man next to me on my left made no movement, so I gave him a little nudge and said, "Come on Jack time to get up." He did not move. He was dead, I then suddenly remembered two days previously in conversation he had said to me that he did not think he would survive the prison camps. The realisation of his words convinced me that he had given up the fight to survive. As I lay there in my weak state during that day I thought about my own situation, his death although commonplace and was happening constantly, did have some effect on me and I began to think that it would end all problems and be an easy way out. I realised in fact that it was easier to die than live. No more struggling and slaving all day under the unrelenting hot tropical sun, weak and constantly suffering from hunger through lack of food, tormented and beaten by our captors, the hateful Japs. No news from the outside world, which would have given us possibly some hope, or news of the progress of the war and eventual release from this terrible existence. In my weakened present state these negative thoughts tempted me to take an easy exit and a peaceful solution to end it all. Yes, it would be easier to die than carry on with this present existence. As I lay on my bed space I compared my state of health and body with those men I used to see when passing through the hospital huts in previous camps, the sight was not pleasant. Men who had been fit and strong British soldiers, were now reduced to physical wrecks, lying there with all their bones showing through their fleshless bodies, their sunken eyes staring and disinterested just waiting for it all to end and relieve them of their suffering, then to be wrapped in their sleeping blanket, or rice sack and buried in a clearing in the jungle just outside the camp along with many others in unmarked graves, after all we are only a number. With these thoughts I must have drifted off to a semi-conscious sleep and had a dream. My parents came to visit me with my family, they also passed on regards from my friends. It was morning when I woke up, my mate had brought me my ration of rice which I managed to eat with a small amount of Goola Malaka. (brown sweat liquid). He asked if I wanted to go the latrines, I said "No I am going to try to get there on my own!" I struggled to get on my feet and out of the tent and stumbled, I walked a bit and crawled my way to the latrine, because I had got there I felt a little better. I returned to the tent a little stronger than when I had left it. As the day progressed I became more strong.

Our health and dress after 18 months as POWs

The following morning I awoke and felt much better and stronger still and I came to the conclusion that my dream had not happened by chance, I again realised that the most important thing at the moment was to survive this hell and one day go home. As the days progressed I regained more strength and was eventually able to return to the working party building the bridge that we had come to build. However, our problems continued. The natives passing through somehow caused an outbreak of Cholera. This disease was the most terrible I have ever experienced. Within forty eight hours the inside is passed out through the back passage and you die. Two men in my tent became infected, two days later I joined a party to help burn their bodies.

The situation became so serious the officers drew up some rules to try and arrest the outbreak. At the place where our food was issued, a fire was lit and over it a large field boiling container was placed filled with water and brought to the boil so that just before food was issued we had to immerse our mess tins for several seconds. This together with the fact that all food consumed had been through the boiling process, infection from this source could not take place.

Above: the Khwae Bridge in a recent photo.

Next page: the same bridge after bombing by allied planes during the war.

It may be worth mentioning that the Japanese provided the minimum of kitchen equipment, which consisted of several round cast iron rice boilers, they looked like giant deep saucers about three feet in diameter and about two feet deep at their centre. these were used for both rice and vegetables. Clay like earth was used to build a thick wall over which the boiler was placed. Once the wall was dry and firm a hole would be made to enable a fire to be lit under the boiler. Dry wood and bamboo would be used as kindle, there was plenty of it in the jungle. Lengths of wood were cut from the jungle and cut to a flat at the end to act as stirrers. We still also had some standard army six gallon boilers and lots of four gallon petrol tins, these ex petrol tins were extremely valuable to us, most of the men had one. we used it for all sorts of purposes, but mostly a quick wash each morning. We could not have carried on without our friend the petrol tin. With the top cut off, two holes would be made to attach a piece of wire to act as a carrying handle. When moving from camp to camp it was no strange site to see men carrying their petrol tin in their hand or fastened to the back pack.

After several more weeks deaths from Cholera began to decline, it seemed that the precautions taken were having results, however, Dysentery, Malaria and tropical ulcers were taking their toll. Tropical ulcers due to the fact that nothing was available to treat them spread rapidly, usually on the legs. The slightest scratch from bamboo developed into a sore within days, it soon became an open wound, nothing stopped it spreading. Within a few weeks the flesh is so eaten away with puss and maggots often the bone was visible. With no treatment or bandages it was impossible to keep flies off the wound. Often nothing could be done in advanced cases but to amputate the limb. Efforts to keep the wound clean were extremely painful, warm saline water did not have any great effect as the medical orderlies had no swabs to clean up the wound, quite often dreadful screams could be heard because they were using a teaspoon to scrape out the puss.

The above shows the layout of a typical jungle cookhouse.

Each morning the agony of those who were fit for work went on, the battle between the MO and the Nips often resulted in the officer getting beaten up. His protests were useless and as long as a man could stand on his two feet he had to go out with the party. Even though the sick would be useless on the working party, they had to go. The Nips wanted a certain number of men each day and that number had to be provided. It was a sort of face saving situation so far as they were concerned. The only thing that mattered in their minds was that the railway had to be built with all speed no matter how many POWs lives were lost in the process.

According to records kept by my parents we, in the prison camps, were not the only ones suffering. Having written countless letters to the War Office and British Red Cross, since February 1942, confirmation as to whether I was still alive or dead was unknown to anyone in the UK. Even as late as April 1943, no positive news had been received, they had in fact received many letters of condolence and sympathy, from all sorts of people and organisations. But during June 1943, with joy, a letter from OIC. Recce Corps Records informed them that official notification from the War Office confirmed that I was a prisoner of war in Malaya.

It will most likely be of interest to readers to see copies of three very important letters received by my parents during this very worrying time in their lives.

WAR ORGANISATION

RL/PE/1.

OF THE

BRITISH RED CROSS SOCIETY and ORDER OF ST. JOHN OF JERUSALEM

President:
HER MAJESTY THE QUEEN.

Grand Prior:
H.R.H. THE DUKE OF GLOUCESTER, K.G.

WOUNDED, MISSING AND RELATIVES DEPARTMENT

Chairman:
THE DOWAGER LADY AMPTHILL, C.I., G.B.E.

TELEPHONE NO.
SLOANE 9696

TELEGRAPHIC ADDRESS:
"WOMIREL, KNIGHTS, LONDON"

9. 4. 43

7 BELGRAVE SQUARE
LONDON, S.W.1

In replying please quote reference:

Re. Pte to R. Gates 4920444 Recce Corps

Dear *Mr. Gates*

We have received your enquiry for news of your *son* and are so sorry to tell you that none has yet reached us about him. Unfortunately, owing to the limited co-operation of the Japanese Government with the International Red Cross Committee at Geneva, we are unable to make our usual enquiries for men who are missing in the Far East. We can only wait until the Japanese Government send us the information which was promised so long ago.

The Japanese Government have recently sent us some names of prisoners in Singapore and Malaya, and though the lists are comparatively short, it does give us reason to hope that the full lists will be sent by them before long. In the meantime, please try not to be too discouraged by the lack of news, as it is thought that the majority of those of whom we still have no information are safe and prisoners of war. You can rest assured that we will let you know as soon as it is possible to send you any news.

With deep sympathy in this long period of suspense,

Yours sincerely,

pp *Margaret Ampthill*

Chairman.

Reply from the Red Cross dated 9th April 1943.

No. 3/R ecce/1/3   Army Form B. 104—83A.
(If replying, please quote
above No.)

RECCE, CORPS,
RECORDS.
3 JUN 1943
II, STRATHEARN R. ..,
EDINBURGH, ..
....Record Office,

....Station.

....19

SIR OR MADAM,

   I have to inform you that a report has been received
from the War Office to the effect that (No.) *4 9 20 444*
(Rank) *Tpr.* ....(Name). *Wilfred R. YATES*
(Regiment) ....*18th RECONNAISSANCE CORPS*...........
is a Prisoner of War *in Japanese hands at*
.............*MALAI camp*...........

   Should any other information be received concerning him, such
information will be at once communicated to you.

   Instructions as to the method of communicating with Prisoners of
War can be obtained at any Post Office.

Mr. W H. Yates.   I am,
       SIR OR MADAM,
252 Sandon Rd,   Your obedient Servant,

Stafford

            Officer in charge of Records.

  IMPORTANT.—Any change of your address should be immediately notified to this
Office. It should also be notified, if you receive information from the soldier above, that
his address has been changed.

Wt.30241/1250 500M. 9/39. KJL/8818 Gp.698/3 Forms/B.104—83A/6

Confirmation from the War Office dated June 3rd 1943,

(next page- Letter from the Red Cross dated 16th September 1943.)

The Forgotten Army page 80

WAR ORGANISATION
OF THE
BRITISH RED CROSS SOCIETY and ORDER OF ST. JOHN OF JERUSALEM

PW/FE/1d/43.

President:
HER MAJESTY THE QUEEN.

Grand Prior:
H.R.H. THE DUKE OF GLOUCESTER, K.G.

PRISONERS OF WAR DEPARTMENT

Chairman:
MAJOR-GENERAL SIR RICHARD HOWARD-VYSE. K.C.M.G., D.S.O.

Deputy Chairman:
J. M. EDDY, C.B.E.
FAR EAST SECTION.
Controller: S. G. KING

TELEPHONE NO.:
REGENT 0111 (5 LINES)

9, PARK PLACE,
ST. JAMES'S STREET,
LONDON, S.W.1

When replying please quote reference: FE/40343.

16.9.43.

Tpr. W.R. Yates.

Dear Mrs Yates,

Thank you for your letter advising us that you have received intimation that *your son* is a prisoner of war in Japanese hands. We are very glad that this news of his safety has at last been received.

Arrangements have been made for the transmission of letters to prisoners of war in the Far East, and the enclosed leaflet will give you full details.

The present position in regard to parcels is given on the back of this letter.

We should like you to know that we shall retain complete records at this office of *your son* and shall be only too pleased to render you every assistance at any time should you either call or write to us. If you write would you kindly quote the above reference as this will enable us to give you prompt attention.

We are so sorry that owing to great pressure of work there has been this delay in writing to you.

Yours sincerely,

P.V.
for CONTROLLER.

It was in fact late June 1943 when we moved to this terrible camp of the Cholera outbreak and we were sure it was brought to the camp by native workers who still passed through daily, to work further north towards the Burma border of the railway. Each day on our way to work on the bridge we would pass several of them lying on or beside the embankment. The Korean guards and Jap engineers would walk as far away from them as possible, they were so scared. We had to take several chunkles with us each morning, on arrival at the site where we were building the bridge, the so called anti cholera party would be picked. Several men would be chosen with one Korean guard, I was chosen on one occasion to join the party. Each of us armed with a chunkle would go back along the embankment to where the bodies of the natives lay, without checking whether they were alive or dead, our guards would not allow us to touch them, after digging a shallow hole, we would drag the body into it with our tools and bamboo poles and replace the earth. During this process, if by any chance we saw a body move we still dug the hole and left it untouched but returned next day to complete the burial. Our feelings of self preservation were completely unmoved by this daily exercise. Life was so cheap in those days. Death was never far away, we got used to it, accepted it. Recent generations of humanity will not understand or believe the depths of misery and hardship endured by everyone involved during the years of the 1939/1945 War.

The Cholera outbreak was making the Nips edgy and very irritable, they were so scared of catching the disease, beatings took place at the slightest provocation. Because of the large number of men with dysentery, small fires had been built and lit at night to help the sick find the latrine more easily. In that camp their hut was not far away, they complained that the fires disturbed their sleep, and the following night at roll call they told the officers to fall out. Several Koreans then arrived armed with bamboo canes, it was obvious they had been drinking to bolster their ego, we were lined up in groups of ten, they then proceeded to go along each line of men beating every one up. Every man in the camp who could stand up was punished and soundly thrashed as they went by. Quite a number of men were knocked out and fell to the ground. Any officer who tried to protest was also punished. The whole dreadful business took over an hour after which the Koreans themselves were completely exhausted. As this was only a small camp with just over 100 British troops and some Dutch troops, who were giving them some problems, we were at the mercy of Korean other ranks who were in charge of us. They were in fact mere coolies before the war and totally unfit to have authority. Most camps had a Gunso in charge, (the rank is equal to a Sergeant in the British army). The opinion of the Japanese and Korean Army as regards POWs is totally different to that of the British Army and other western countries. They are taught that to surrender would be considered as an act of treason and therefore, the British soldier was the lowest form of life and therefore we were treated as such.

Since the Dutch joined us in the camps, most of them came from Java and therefore knew quite a lot of plants that grow in the jungle, we were shown a plant that looked very much like spinach, some sort of root tuber was also edible. As we were then getting a little meat we were able to supplement our vegetable ration with a jungle stew. This together with regular calls by the Thai's in their barges who were always eager to make a few dollars sold us duck eggs and other things. As these purchases helped to keep us a little fitter our captors turned a blind eye whenever the barges pulled into the river bank. However, we eventually found out that after our purchases had been made, the Nips would go to the boats and demand a free 'presento' as a commission for allowing them to sell their products to us.

August 1943 arrived and the work on the embankment and bridge that I had worked on was moving ahead quite fast, the Nips were screaming and yelling at us from dawn to dusk, hitting out at the least sign of slackness. Breakfast was now taken before dawn and we were out on the road and off to work just as it was getting light. The bridge we were building was eight kilometres away from the camp, so every one had to walk sixteen kilometres in addition to a very strenuous hard days work. The walk back to camp was no more than a disorganised strenuous limp, our agony and weakness seemed to bond into a type of closer relationship with one another, the stronger more able bodied never hesitated to help a mate who seemed to be in distress, it was not a strange sight to often see men literally being carried, being so tired it was often dark when we arrived back at camp. I of course continued with my miserable job with my irritable Elephant and Thai. driver who could not care less about my weakness. He would never do anything to give me the slightest bit of help and often turned a deaf ear to my constant bawling to move the animal how I wanted it to enable me to attaché its hauling harness to whatever I had to drag to the site of the bridge.

At this time there was still a lack of news from the outside world or from home, just rumours, which generally got passed around to the extent that everyone who passes the news on exaggerated it out of all proportion. So eager everyone of us was and keen and interested to hear the latest of what was being passed around. We were all aware that there was the odd secret radio buried in a can and known only to its owner, which was brought out of hiding once in a blue moon to get the latest news. When passed on, no one tried to find out where the news came from and it was always mixed with rumour, so as not to get the men too excited, but at the same time it gave us a lift and enabled us to soldier on. Readers may not understand really how much a bit of good news did, to bolster our spirits and gave us something to discuss as regards to how much longer we had to suffer this terrible existence. There was no doubt that the Nips would not hesitate to shoot anyone found with such equipment as a radio. Rigorous searches often took place, I think they sensed that we somehow got bits of news but were never successful in discovering how and where it came from.

It was whilst at this camp that two Dutch soldiers tried to escape. Goodness knows why, we all realised that there was a price on our heads, although not much, but enough to tempt a native to give us away and the distance and jungle they would have to travel through to freedom was virtually an impossibility. However, they attempted it. After two weeks in the jungle they returned and gave themselves up. We were all herded out and told by the Gunso of their crime against Nipon for which they were to be beheaded in front of all of us, as an example of what would happen to anyone else who tried to escape. They were made to dig their graves before execution, after which the Gunso drew his sword from its scabbard, we all then knew that he was not bluffing and intended chopping their heads off. This is done in a mighty downward and swirling action with both hands gripping the sword. They could often be seen practising this action outside their billet. The process of beheading someone to them was no more than a ritual. Like all their race, they were completely indifferent to human suffering. However, our officer in charge with great risk to himself confronted the Gunso, saluted and begged him to allow all troops to fall out and not be forced to witness the execution as it would be very bad for moral and affect our ability to work. He stood for something like a whole minute which seemed ages, swore at him and struck him, then said all men go. Our officer again saluted, turned and ordered us to fall out. We found out later that the two Dutchmen were in a terrible mess in pools of blood when allowed to be buried by their fellow prisoners.

He tried to escape.

It was late August 1943 when we heard the news that we were to leave the terrible camp Qui-ichi and move south, the bridge had been finished and we hoped to get away from the sadistic barbaric Korean swines, who at the slightest misdemeanour never hesitated to take great pleasure in beating everyone up that was anywhere near them. Thank goodness they were just our guards and had no control over us whilst working. The Japanese engineers made us work very hard, but there was very little beating up on the job. An act of terrible brutality occurred a few days before we left the camp. The Dutch POWs always seemed to suffer the worst treatment. One of them forgot to salute when passing the Korean guardhouse. He was immediately tied to a tree nearby and severely beaten with a rifle butt, we could hear his screams way off but kept well out of the way. Apparently he caught hold of one of the guard's arms in a vain effort to protect himself, which would be considered as an act of resistance, the result was that the punishment was increased to both the head and body. He was beaten to a pulp and covered in blood, this was one of the worst thrashings we experienced during our period of captivity. I am pleased to say that we heard that he survived the punishment. Soon afterwards we had some good news, apparently the Korean guards went to the Japanese engineers camp to ask if they could shoot the Dutchman because he had offered resistance to them. As stated previously the Japanese hated the Koreans and knew more or less what was going on and reported the incident to their superiors. The outcome was that guards who took part in the beating had to report to the Jap HQ. We did not find out what happened to them but they did not return to the camp and their replacements were a very subdued lot. A Japanese sergeant was appointed to take over the camp, from then on, there were not so many beatings.

Chapter VIII

The End Of The Speedo

It was in September 1943 when we moved to our new camp, it was only a small one and the Jap engineers have no separate camp they were in with us with a sergeant in charge, so our lives were not at the mercy of the three Korean guards. The camp was just an open space beside the river and we had to set to work and build a couple of huts. As we were told that there was only one bridge to be built, it was decided to erect just enough protection to keep the rain out for the few weeks we were going to be there. The worst job was always the latrine that had to be deep enough for the obvious reasons. It was at this camp that a rumour quickly spread around that the allies had landed in Italy on September 9th 1942 and that a very large and powerful force of tanks, guns and stores, the biggest yet in the war had landed at Naples. The news bucked every one up and we all thought that maybe the war would be over by Christmas. We knew that a radio set existed and buried below ground in one of the camps near us, but no one knew which, it did not matter as long as we got some news. This was the first for some considerable time. To be caught with a radio would be considered a most serious offence and certain death, therefore the words 'radio set' were never mentioned. If it was talked about we would say 'the birds are singing again.' Readers will realise that living in the jungle away from all civilisation, to get some news from the outside world was a real life saver and gave us something to talk about other than to reminiscing about food enjoyed in the past before captivity and anything else that came to mind, in fact anything to take our minds away from our present existence.

It turned out that we had moved to this place to repair a bridge and not build it. We found the railway line had been completed and during the days that followed several trains passed through to finish track laying further north. It was also noticeable that work continued on at somewhat slower pace, the Nip engineers seemed more relaxed and not rushing us around shouting "speedo speedo", a further bonus our camp was positioned alongside the bridge and therefore no weary miles to walk. The food had also improved a little over the past few weeks as we had been allowed some extra meat, this helped enormously, the extra protein seemed to reduce the number of men falling sick, although we would be very lucky if we got more than about four very small pieces of meat in our evening meal.

Early October 1943 we were told that the railway was finished and that we would be going south for a rest. Maybe we would be going south, but for a rest, I would think not. Trains were now passing through the camp daily in both directions and on the day we were told to pack up, believe it or not a train with a number of empty wagons stopped at our camp and we were told to climb aboard and that we would be going back to Hindato. The journey south was extremely interesting, although tightly packed in the wagons, we were able to sit down and enjoy the magnificent scenery that was a misery to us when walking through it. The jungles of Thailand when viewed from a train are like being in a world centuries old. Mountains of rock protruding above the jungle canopy. Mile after mile, we crossed high viaducts and bridges, some of which we had built ourselves. There were vast and miniature waterfalls, cascading and rushing down over rocks and land on its way down to the wide and deep Khwae River below. A river which, until we arrived, had been the only source and means of travelling between Bangkok and the Burma border of Thailand. Passing through deep gorges and cuttings we realised the enormous amount of labour and loss of life that must have been used during the twelve months we had been involved in the building and making the railway possible. No machines or mechanical excavators had been used, just the bare hands of POWs with hand tools. It was eventually worked out that the railway cost the life of someone equal to each sleeper laid. The journey also made us realise how hopeless it would be to try to escape.

We eventually arrived at Hindato camp to find that it had become much bigger than when we left it some months earlier. There was now a separate hospital hut, a canteen stocked with fruit, tobacco, eggs etc, if you had money to buy. We noticed a fenced off area which contained several cattle, although terribly thin, indicated that we would be sure of getting some meat in our ration. Our first meal that night was far better than anything we had been given for many months. The next day we were told by the Nips that we had been sent there for a rest and would only need to do camp duties. We thought Christmas had come early, but we did not really believe what they said, time would tell.

The days that followed were some of the happiest spent as prisoners in the jungle. In between camp duties we found time to play football with a ball borrowed from the Nips. We then found out that they had hatched a plot to give a good impression to the outside world. They instructed us to arrange a football match with a prize for the winning team. As soon as the game started they arrived with cameras and took snaps of the game, to compound the farce they also placed a table with some empty beer bottles and included it in the pictures. The photographs would show happy contented POWs playing football and having drinks of beer, with beautiful scenery in their jungle camp. Nothing could be further from the truth.

Our period of relaxation did not last, early one morning a party of men were marched off to meet a train from which they unloaded lots of axes and cross cut saws to be brought back into our camp. Next morning all the fittest were paraded and told we were to go into the jungle to cut fire wood to fuel the engines of trains which were now passing through daily loaded with Japanese soldiers on their way we assumed to fight in Burma. Now we were having to illegally help the Japanese war effort. In recent weeks at night time when there was a moon, we thought we could faintly hear the hum of planes in the distance, but with the absence of any news it was most annoying not knowing what was going on in the war.

The wood cutting job was very strenuous and difficult, not being trained for this work, we experienced all sorts of difficulties. The instructions were, first to fell the chosen tree remove all branches, saw the trunk into half metre lengths then chop these half metre lengths into pieces to enable them to be fed into the engine firebox. There was no supervision for this work, we were left entirely on our own, but the catch was, we had to produce one cubic metre of stacked fire wood per man daily. We could not go back to camp until every stack had been literally checked with a measure. That first day was a disaster some had not finished when it began to get dark. The biggest problem was getting the tree to fall to the ground, as many of them became entangled in the canopy at the felling stage. Some trees had wood that was so hard such as teak it was impossible to cut them. When we eventually arrived back at camp the Australians in each hut called all in the hut together and gave a short talk on the felling of trees, most were experienced in this sort of work, they suggested and organised us to work in groups of four and if possible try to arrange to have an Australian in as many groups as possible. the following day in agreement with the Nips we organised ourselves in fours, each group collecting two axes and a crosscut saw. We asked if we could keep the set of tools relative to our group so that we could keep them well sharpened. On the job we would look for a suitable tree that would fall un-entangled by surrounding vegetation, so trees that were near to the open space of the rail track would be suitable to tackle. The decision on a particular tree was never easy as it had to fall precisely in the right direction. To do this it was necessary to chop a 'v' shaped cut at a suitable chopping height into the tree in the direction we wanted and hoped it would fall. As the cut out was made, sometimes the tree would begin to lean a little in the direction we wished it to fall, we then, with the two handed cross-cut saw begin to saw into the trunk on the opposite side of the 'v' cut and slightly above to ensure that the tree would continue to lean and not bind on the saw. As soon as we heard the tree crack we would quickly withdraw the saw and run well clear and hope the tree would fall clear to the ground. The branches then had to be removed in order to cut up the trunk in half metre lengths, then chop each half metre length into pieces, and finally make a stack four cubic square alongside the rail-track. (One cubic metre for each man.) Each stack was measured religiously by the Nips before anyone could return to camp. Some groups had to be assisted as the tasks never ran smoothly. As the days went by we began to become wise as to which trees to look for. One specie in particular was very much like Balsa and the saw went through it like a knife through butter. If we were lucky enough to find one we could complete our task by early afternoon, then help others.

Week after week we carried on cutting timber for the engines. Day after day the task began to become more and more difficult, having to walk farther away to continue stacking timber further along the track. The month of November 1943 arrived and passed. Many men unfit for work had been steadily moved south to the hospital camp at Kanchanburi, we all, however, still suffered regular bouts of Malaria and other problems, but the death rate had considerably fallen as most of the chronically sick had been moved out. the food which, even at that time was only just enough to keep one alive without the strenuous work we had to do. The number of cattle in the pen soon dwindled there was very little meat on them. They provided a little meat in the evening meal every other day. It should be said however, that the food we were having in that camp was far better than any other camp we had worked from during the months we had been slaving on the railway.

Rumours began to spread around the camp that somewhere in Thailand was a stack of mail which we should have received. What a lift it would have been to get some news from home. We had recently been allowed to complete another card which, to ensure that its onward transmission, did not dare to mention our poor condition. As far as they were concerned we were fit and well.

As the days passed by work in the jungle became less and less, as the distance to walk and fell trees became too great to be worthwhile. The camp grew bigger and bigger, as more troops were moved in, after finishing their appointed tasks at various other camps on the railway. Soon another Christmas loomed on the horizon, there were rumours of another move south. The Nips said that they were going to give us some extra food at Christmas. We all wondered why nothing had been received from the Red Cross. When Christmas eventually came, we had a very good time for once. First the Nips allowed us a full two days holiday. We did get extra food and the cook house staff rose to the occasion, but the highlight went to a very kind Chinese, who arrived with a boat load of all sorts of food two days before Christmas. He was selling it of course, but he had brought all sorts of food, such as eggs, bacon, sausage, ham, cakes. Other ranks could not afford much but the officers had a heyday. The smell of bacon and eggs being cooked on Xmas morning, by those who could afford it drove everyone else mad. Christmas day finished up with a concert. It was one of the best I have ever seen, with so many people in the camp, there was no shortage of talent. Even the Nips who came to have a look seemed to enjoy it. We all went to sleep that night more contented than at any time as prisoners. all of us without doubt, wondered if it would be our last in captivity. Only time would tell.

January 1944 arrived and at last that long awaited mail arrived. It was good to hear from the folks at home, everyone seemed to be in good spirits. My thoughts were with those families who had sent letters to their loved ones, not knowing that they would be amongst the many thousands that had died; they, without doubt, would not have received the bad news.

Although the work on the railway had finished, the Nips still found us plenty to do in camp. Huts had to be repaired, we also spent quite a lot of time digging monsoon drains around the huts, which helped to keep the camp from getting water logged during heavy storms. When it rains there, believe me it rains. The wind will increase to hurricane strength, as many men as possible will climb onto the roof of their hut and hang on the ridge to give weight to prevent it from being blown away. At the same time torrential rain lashes down continuously. It does not take long before the camp is temporarily flooded. Luckily when the rain stops, it soon drains away and the sun dries everything up very quickly.

Two orderlies returning from a trip down river with a party of sick, brought some bad news back with them. Apparently, during a search the

Nips had found a radio receiver and the four officers involved, who were apparently British had been taken to the guard room and badly beaten up. Two of them had been beaten all through the night and screams could be heard through out the camp. The thrashing was so severe, they died. The other two, after their severe punishment were sent to Singapore gaol, which we understood from rumours would be a fate worse than death. Even to this day, more than fifty years on, I cannot believe that the Japanese have changed from their wild, barbaric trait. On another occasion, in another camp, one of the British POWs caught the dreaded cholera. The Nip in charge ordered the man to be shot. British officers tried in vain to stop the execution. The man would have died anyway, no one unluckily having caught it, survived the dreaded cholera outbreak.

The eventual move south took place in March 1994. It was sudden, no one realised we were to leave Hindato until the day before, and the following morning found us being tightly packed into trucks for our journey to a camp called Nonpladok II. This camp was situated only about two miles from Bampong, the camp we entered, after our journey from Singapore to start work on the railway. The camp was very large with well built huts, out of the jungle, in open populated countryside. Another large camp but separated from us, stood alongside the railway track, with lots of railway sidings, full of loaded trucks. This camp was called Nonpladok I. Our new camp also had a reasonably equipped hospital. I did not realise when first seeing it, that before long I would be paying a visit to the part partitioned off which was used for minor operations. The hospital had its own staff, from what I saw they were needed, it was overcrowded with chronically sick men just skin and bone, how they kept alive I will never know. They had been in the camp for some time, obviously sent here from the working camps up river. Speaking to one of the orderlies he told me that he understood that the death rate of POWs on the railway had reached fifteen thousand. I thought 'what a diabolical waste of life!' The one big difference with this camp, we were now no longer near the river, all water had to be pumped from underground, so our treasured possession, the ex four gallon petrol can came into full use again. Our work here turned out to be the erection of more huts and digging monsoon drains as the camp had to be made much bigger to take other POWs returning from the camps up country. The work was just as strenuous, as now there was not a bit of shade, we were working under a burning hot sun all day. Day after day we carried on building huts and digging drains and latrines, gradually more and more troops came into the camp to occupy the huts we had built. April 1944 came and we were allowed to complete another printed card home. As the camp filled we heard another rumour that a number of men were to be sent to Japan. No doubt something would have to happen soon, as the camp had in the region of about four thousand men with really not a lot to do. Most of work in the camp was being done without Korean or Nip supervision, as it was for our own benefit. At least fewer beatings took place and we were much happier without their presence. The food was considerably better. The stews were more like a stew, with a little more meat and veg. This situation was because we turned the open ground around the camp into a vegetable garden. We even grew some tobacco plants. At least if nothing else, we were getting a little more food. Perhaps it may be worth mentioning that at that particular time, my sole possessions consisted of one army blanket, a ground sheet to lie on, no clothing whatsoever, except a 'jap happy,' (the name we gave to a loin cloth always worn by the Japs under their trousers.) This consisted of a piece of material of any sort, about two feet long and about ten inches wide with a tape attached to one end to fasten round my waist. The piece of cloth would be brought forward between the legs and folded over the tape at the front. These 'jap happies' did not last with the constant perspiration and dust. I washed mine out every other day, in doing so, I would examine it around the tape and kill off any body lice and eggs between my thumb nails. I had no footwear, my boots had worn out over a year ago. All I had was mess tin and spoon, a rusty milk tin with a handle made of wire, and a four gallon petrol tin. I was also able to keep my army issue haversack, which I used as a pillow. I now really cannot believe how we managed to survive, and I am sure that anyone reading this will have great difficulty in believing and understanding the terrible uncivilised conditions in which those of us who, with no more than sheer bloody determination, lived through it and survived, those three and a half years of hell.

At that time however, our spirits had begun to rise. Bits of news had been passed around that the war was going our way. Major General Wingate and his 'chindits' were giving the Japanese a thrashing in Burma. We were pleased they were getting some of their own medicine. We also heard the occasional plane overhead. Our guards did not appear to be so happy, beating became less and less. The trains passing through going north were filled with very young Japanese soldiers with solemn looks on their faces. None ever returned.

On display for tourists at Kanchanburi

THAI – BURMA RAILWAY LINE

1.   DURING THE SECOND WORLD WAR THE JAPANESE ARMY CONSTRUCTED A MILITARY RAILWAY LINE BRANCHING OFF THE SOUTHERN LINE AT NONG PLADUK STATION. KM. 64+196. THIS LINE CROSSED OVER THE RIVER KWAI YAI AT KANCHANABURI. TRAVERSED ALONG THE BANK OF KWAI NOI RIVER. CUT ACROSS THE THAI-BURMA BORDER AT CHEDI SAM ONG. CONTINUED ON INTO BURMA AND JOINED THE BURMA RAILWAY LINE AT THANBYUZAYAT. THE TOTAL LENGTH OF LINE CONSTRUCTED WAS 415 KMS., BEING IN THAILAND 303.95 KMS. AND IN BURMA 111.05 KMS.

2.   CONSTRUCTION WORK STARTED IN OCTOBER 1942. A YEAR LATER ON 23 OCTOBER 1943 RAIL LAYING WAS COMPLETED. ABOUT 60,000 MEN CONSISTING OF INDIAN, BURMESE, MALAYSIAN, INDONESIAN. CHINESE AND THAI LABOURERS AS WELL AS PRISONERS OF WAR TOOK PART IN THE CONSTRUCTION WORK.

3.   THE DIESEL POWER TRACTION CAR SHOWN HERE WAS USED DURING THE CONSTRUCTION. IT COULD BE RUN EITHER ON ROAD OR RAILWAY TRACK. THE ROAD WHEELS WOULD BE LOWERED INTO POSITION WHEN REQUIRED. THE STEAM LOCOMOTIVE SHOWN WAS EMPLOYED FOR MILITARY TRANSPORT SERVICE ON THIS LINE.

4.   IN SPEEDING UP CONSTRUCTION WORK THE JAPANESE ARMY BUILT A TEMPORARY RAILWAY BRIDGE ACROSS THE RIVER KWAI YAI DOWNSTREAM CLOSED TO THE EXISTING BRIDGE. AFTER COMPLETION OF THE EXISTING BRIDGE COMPOSING OF 11 STEEL SPANS WITH THE REST OF TIMBER SPANS, THE TEMPORARY BRIDGE WAS DISMANTLED TO EASE OFF RIVER TRAFFIC INCONVENIENCE. THREE STEEL SPANS NOS. 4,5,6 WERE DAMAGED BY ALLIED BOMBING DURING THE WAR PERIOD. AFTER TAKING OVER THE LINE THE STATE RAILWAY OF THAILAND REPLACED THE THREE DAMAGED SPANS WITH TWO STEEL SPANS AND CHANGED ALL TIMBER SPANS AT THE FAR END WITH SIX STEEL SPANS.

5.   WHEN THE WAR CAME TO AN END IN 1945 THE BRITISH ARMY DISMANTLED 3.95KMS. OF TRACK AT THE THAI – BURMA BORDER. THE REMAINING LENGTH OF 300 KMS. WAS HANDED OVER TO THE STATE RAILWAY OF THAILAND IN 1947. WITH DUE AND CAREFUL CONSIDERATION IN REGARD TO TRANSPORT ECONOMIC AS WELL AS OTHER ASPECTS. THE STATE RAILWAY OF THAILAND WAS AUTHORISED TO DISMANTLE THE TRACK FROM THE END OF THE LINE TO NAM TOK STATION AND TO UPGRADE THE REMAINING LENGTH OF 130.204 KMS. TO NONG PLADUK STATION CONFORMING TO OPERATIONAL PERMANENT WAY STANDARD. SUBSEQUENTLY, THE SECTION BETWEEN NONG PLADUK AND KANCHANABURI STATIONS WAS OFFICIALLY OPENED TO TRAFFIC ON 24 JUNE 1949. BETWEEN KANCHANABURI AND WANG PHO STATIONS ON 1 APRIL 1952 AND THE LAST SECTION FROM WANG PHO TO NAM TOK STATIONS ON 1 JULY 1958.

STATE RAILWAY OF THAILAND.

Our situation further improved in May 1944, at last after two years some Red Cross parcels arrived in camp. They had without doubt, been held up by the Japanese. Most of it went into the cookhouse. We did get a bar of soap each and a few cigarettes. There was also some drugs and medical supplies, which we considered to be most valuable. We appreciated that the Japs would not be prepared to release what the vast Red Cross Empire would be able to provide. If they had, our standard of living would have been higher than theirs.

It seemed that at that time, having toiled and completed the job of building the railway, our captors became a little more bearable. In some ways in their own peculiar fashion, they too tried to make believe that they were our friends. A notice board was erected and from time to time we would read amusing pidgin English messages, one of which I would like to include in my story. The exact wording I personally cannot remember, but luckily I was able to obtain it from a fellow POW. after release. The message went as follows:-

"We Japs will help you our good friends as you help us and all the time we gratitude to you. We observe that your work is very business and you work very diligent. Nipon army is very different, Nip general severity, very gentle, but in army strokes is very frequently. Don't anxiety one or two strokes. We all Jap soldiers was taken plenty of strokes the early time of entering Jap army. Any time you are good and the Jap soldiers are no good Jap Sgt. is sure to scold you. When you get any you must bear, you must have knowledge of Jap soldiers harshness as you know." They were trying to write an apology for the beatings that had taken place. We knew that if they did anything wrong, their punishment was to be stood to attention and receive several blows across the face administered by a higher rank, usually their sergeant. But I should add that our punishment was by far, very much more severe than theirs.

The party of men which had to be the fittest had been picked, to go to Japan, I was on the list to go and would be moving out in about one week. However, I had what would be considered now as a very fortunate, but at that time very unfortunate nasty accident. One day working in a drain with chunkles, I suddenly felt something strike me a viscous blow on the lower part of my back, right on my spine. I swung round in anger, but in doing so my head began to swim, and I thought I was going to pass out, there was blood everywhere. The man working immediately behind me had accidentally caught me with his chunkle. I assume I must have taken a step back for him to have caught me. Several mates dragged me out of the drain, which was about three feet deep. They quickly carried me to the hospital hut and into the part used for operations. Someone had already gone to find the MO, who was there almost as soon as I was. They put me on the bamboo table tummy down, the MO took one look and said: "What a bloody mess, how did this happen." I could not answer. He immediately began to clean the wound, and I offered a prayer to thank God for the medical supplies that had recently arrived. He stitched up the wound which I understood to be about five inches long, but deep and down to the backbone. After stitching he padded the wound and finished with quite a lot of bandage round my waist. He slapped my bottom and said "That will do for the time being." He then had a thought and said, "I suppose you are on the party for Japan." I said, "Yes." He then said, "Those stitches will have to come out before you leave, come to see me before you go." Four days later I reported to him that we were to move off the following morning. His feelings were that it was too soon to remove them, but after some deliberation, he decided there was no alternative, he then took out the stitches and applied a new bandage. He advised me to try to find some one in my party who could replace the dressings.

The next morning I joined the others all packed up and ready to leave. My two best mates stood with me, waiting for the Nips to come and march us off. As they came along the rank to count us, one of them stopped in front of me and looked at the bandage round my waist, turned me round and pulled off the pad and bandage to have a look. He uttered the words "English soldier, dammy, dammy, no good, beoki," (Japanese for sick.) after a discussion with several other Nips, he came back to me, pulled me away from my mates, and said: "English soldier no good stay." I was not going. I now cannot recall my exact thoughts at that particular time. I was probably sorry at losing my mates, but at the same time relieved, not knowing what conditions the party would have to suffer, either on their journey to Japan, or what was in store for them, if they got there. As I write this since my return from captivity, I can state that they were cooped up in a hot stinking hold for most of their journey by ship, on a dangerous trip and with the possibility of coming under fire from allied planes. I understand from reports, that there were several ships loaded with prisoners that did not make it to Japan, as under attack they were battened down in the hold and therefore, perished with the ship. Those that survived the journey were made to work in mines. My best mate suffered with a bad chest for the rest of his life and it was partly to blame for his death.

With hindsight, my accident happened to stop me from going to Japan. Although I had a nasty wound, it was probably for the best. On reporting back to the MO, he was surprised to find that I was still in camp. He also said "What a pity," that he could not stitch it up again. Sadly within several days, having to work, the wound opened up, what a mess it was. Thank goodness we had some medical supplies, without them it is doubtful I would have survived. It took weeks to heal from the inside. Today fifty-five years on, it is still very tender, and I cannot bear anyone to even tap me on that spot. It sends a very strange shock straight up my spine.

Within the next few weeks several parties had left the camp on their way to Japan. There was now very little to do, other than maintenance in the camp and gardening, which was flourishing with all sorts of vegetables. We even grew peanuts. As there were such a lot of flies around and they seemed to be on the increase, the Nips gave an order that every man had to catch thirty flies a day. They also said 'any man who could hand in a quinine bottle full, would be paid thirty five cents.' For some weeks the task was easy, but to fill a quinine bottle took many hours. Eventually it was very difficult to even catch thirty. Then someone had a brain waive, by mixing dried tea leaves with the flies, they soon had a bottle full. So even though there were very few flies about, plenty of bottles were being handed in at thirty five cents a time. This went on for some time until the Nips realised there were no flies about and stopped the payments.

As the camp was virtually very close to the local community, we regularly became up to date with news from the outside world. Local papers had been smuggled in written in Thai and Chinese. Although Japanese controlled, it was possible to read between the lines. The result was that our spirits rose to the extent that if the assumptions were correct, we could be free by Christmas.

It was from these papers that we read about 'D day' Landings along the Normandy coastline by British and American troops, early on the morning of the 6th of June 1944. They were under the command of General Eisenhower and had subsequently been successfully moving inland. By August 1944 it was noticed that allied planes passing overhead, had become a regular daily occurrence; a battery of anti aircraft guns had been placed just outside our camp. Each day as the planes passed over they would open up in the hope of shooting some down. I cannot recall them hitting a single one. We did however, hope that the allied planes realised that two POW camps stood beside the railway sidings.

We did not have long to wait to find out. It was early September 1944; I had retired to my bed space to go to sleep when I heard planes overhead and almost immediately after, some terrible explosions which shook the whole camp. All hell was let loose, I jumped up ran out of the hut and dropped into the monsoon drain alongside. The ack ack opened up we could hear the planes passing over the camp, they were attacking the railway sidings and goods yard. Then it seemed one plane came from another direction and dropped its bombs, there was one hell of an explosion very close I could smell the cordite. Instinctively, I felt myself all over to feel if there was any blood, but I was OK thank God. I lay in the drain waiting and expecting more bombs to fall, but the drone of the planes gradually died away. Climbing out of the trench, I and many others ran through the camp towards the brightly lit sky caused by a fire that was raging. The bombs had fallen between two huts in Nonpladok I. We saw men running about carrying other men. We were powerless to help as the two camps were divided off by a fence. The Japanese never allowed infiltration between camps, whenever two camps happened to be alongside each other.

The next morning we had orders to form a grave digging party. Collecting suitable tools we marched off towards the other camp, at least we would be able to see at first hand the damage and loss of life the bombs had caused. Entering the camp we could see that two huts had gone, others each side had been badly damaged, one of which was used by the officers. Ninety-eight bodies of POWs had been laid out in lines in an open space in the camp. We found out that this had been done in the hope that if a spotter plane came over, to check out their success or otherwise, it would see that many men had been killed. We also found out that almost as many men had been injured, but non fatally. The talk was that one plane decided to attack in the opposite direction from the camps, with the result that its bombs had missed the sidings, to fall in the camp. We assumed the planes were American. It was a very sad day, we dug one large grave to bury all of the dead together. For a day or two afterwards we went to sleep each night wondering if we were going to get more raids. Although allied planes passed over almost every day, they only attacked the siding if there was anything worthwhile destroying. The camp was also hit again and several more POWs lost their lives. The attacks were then taking place in the day time and we could see the planes quite clearly, from our now much deeper drains, which we had turned into trenches alongside our huts.

Chapter IX

The Beginning Of The End

By November 1944, my wound had healed quite well, but it was a very tender spot. I tried to keep it covered as much as possible with a pad supplied by the medics. I was always aware of it and tried to protect it as much as possible. It was during November that I had to join a number of men to move to another camp. This time no officers were allowed in the party and it was under the command of a Sergeant Major. On the way, unknown to us we stopped at the large base camp at Kanchanburi. At first we thought we were going there to stay. It was much better than any camp in Thailand. Being the base camp it was well supplied with food although still inadequate. There was a good hospital where most of the Red Cross supplies were kept. I would have been quite happy to stay there until release, but after a few days rest we were off again. A short journey on the train to a camp at Nakom Kni, very close to Nakom Paton. The camp was some distance from the railway line, and although we could still hear planes passing overhead, we were in no danger as they would have no reason to bomb a prison camp. Our work involved a daily walk for about two miles, then dig into a hillside to form a number of short tunnels. Rumours again started to be passed around the camp. News that the Japanese war effort had been under pressure and that they were loosing the battle in Burma, their attitude towards us also changed, beatings became quite rare, except for what they considered a serious offence. They tended to leave us alone as much as possible, so as the war appeared to be going against them, we began to think that they would, before the end, shoot everyone and bury us in the holes we were digging. After all remember, no officers were allowed to come with us.

On the brighter side we enjoyed Christmas, with several days rest and for once we managed to go through the day without any rice which was most enjoyable. The cookhouse did us proud with the extra food allowed from Red Cross supplies. The next few months that followed from January 1945 passed uneventfully, we continued to dig the holes in the hillside with not the slightest idea what they were going to be used for, we never did find out.

In late June 1945, I with several other POWs, had been ordered to replace part of our hut damaged in a storm. Whilst climbing to re-tie a new cross piece of bamboo I slipped slightly and scratched my right leg below my knee, it was nothing, I hardly noticed it. Within days it looked very angry inflamed and sore. The only treatment available was saline dressings, but they did not have any significant effect and soon I realised it had developed into the dreaded tropical ulcer. The thought of what had happened to other men with ulcers, made me very worried. The ulcer grew day by day and filled with puss, which had to be swabbed away daily. There were no pain killers to help, the treatment was extremely painful, but it had to be done, to try and stop it getting bigger, even with treatment it still continued to grow. By August 1945 it had reached over two and a half inches in diameter, and was quite deep, but I still had to go out to work.

One morning, we had finished breakfast and hung around waiting for Nips to come and fetch us from their camp, which was about a mile away. They never arrived, but the Koreans were still walking round their sentry road around the camp. This road was quite a high embankment around the camp; it was already there when we first arrived and acted as a camp perimeter wall, although it would not keep us in, but we had no wish to go beyond it anyway.

After hanging around for a while, we sensed that something was going on and returned to our huts, shortly someone came in and told us to go out on parade, as I emerged from my hut, everyone from the other huts came out and formed up in the open space. We stood around with not the slightest idea what was going on. After some minutes, our camp commander, the RSM, (Regimental Sergeant Major) emerged from the Korean guard room. He stood in front of us and without showing any emotion shouted: "The war is over, we are free men." For a moment there was a deathly quiet. He repeated the words, and suddenly everyone was cheering. Someone dashed into a hut and emerged with a Union Jack. God knows how he had kept it. He attached it to a bamboo pole and hoisted it up. Everyone cheered again, a lump came into my throat and I began to shed tears, looking round everyone was doing the same. We were all so full of emotion, and experienced a terrific feeling of relief. Someone started to sing "God Save The King," then everyone joined in, we were all singing at the top of our voices with tears streaming down our faces. The historical announcement made by the RSM took place at precisely 11 am on the morning of Friday 17th of August 1945. Although I have said that there were no officers in the camp, we were allowed a Padre, he was an Australian and after the emotion had subsided a little, he conducted a short service of thanksgiving.

What a change an hour can make to a man who had suffered three and a half years of privation and a death dealing existence handed out by our captors, the uncivilised, barbaric soldiers of The Imperial Japanese Army. Men were running around, uncaring about their skinny starved bodies, laughing and joking, slapping one another on the back. The feeling of utter relief was out of this world.

A few of the lads with theatrical backgrounds decided to arrange a concert that evening and use the Korean sentry road as a stage, but the guards, who had kept out of the way since morning stopped us from using it, so it was postponed. That first night of freedom, when it was time to go to bed we were all so keyed up and excited, it was hours before we could get to sleep. The next two days passed uneventfully. The Korean guards had disappeared, they now had no power or authority any more, thank goodness. It was quite a change and pleasant feeling to be able to wander about out of camp at will. The Thai locals attitude changed dramatically. We were freely offered food and fruit, but as there was just the normal rations in camp, we had to continue with the meagre rice diet until someone came to rescue us. We were now virtually stranded, not knowing from where our next supply of food was coming. The concert eventually took place on the second evening of freedom, it was most enjoyable and helped to pass the time, and looking forward to someone taking steps to move us away from our present miserable conditions of living, but happy state of mind.

We had not long to wait, on the third day we heard the drone of a plane in the distance, the sound grew louder and we all ran out of our huts to look. It came towards the camp rather low, it was a large American transporter and as it circled our camp the rear door opened and we could see two men in the plane, we shouted and waived, they waived back. The plane banked and began to rise and move away, our spirits dropped. But then it turned round to face the camp as it approached, a jeep dropped from the plane, followed by two men. Their parachutes opened and they floated to the ground precisely in the open space in front of the huts. They were dressed in full battle order, armed complete with radio sets. What a reception we gave them, they looked very embarrassed. They told us planes were on the way to us with food and clothing. Sure enough the following morning we again, heard planes approaching and ran out to watch, they came in very low no more than about a hundred feet above the ground, as they passed over the camp open space, they pushed out very large almost square hessian covered bales. Without any thought of being crushed, men began to run across the open space towards them and move them, luckily no one was hurt. The RSM stepped in and some organisation was restored. Eventually we were each issued with one set of KD, (khaki drill) i.e. one pair of shorts, a shirt, socks and boots. We also had some soap and a towel. One bale consisted of a complete set of medical supplies. I was very thankful as I was able to get some decent treatment for my ulcer. All the food dropped was taken to the cookhouse, to be issued at meal times. Some organisation then had to take place, to ensure discipline, after the excitement of those first few days.

The two Americans had been given some space in one of our huts, where they set up a radio station to keep in touch with the outside world. In conversation they gave us lots of news about the war ending in Europe. They told us that Adolf Hitler had committed suicide about 2nd of May 1945, and that Field Marshall Montgomery had attended the signing of the surrender of the Germans after capitulation on the 4th of May 1945.

We were also told that Japan had been given the chance to surrender in July 1945. As they did not respond, there was no alternative, a very large area of their county had been wiped out with atom bombs dropped during the first week of August 1945. Eighty thousand people were killed instantly, which no doubt resulted in their capitulation and of course our release. The Americans arrival had taken place, to make contact with whoever was making the arrangements for our welfare, and subsequent move to civilisation. The second night after their arrival, I had been asleep for some time when I heard someone making a noise, getting up and going outside to see what was going on, a group of men were shouting and pointing, I was just in time to see the Americans jump into their Jeep and drive out of camp. Asking the group what was going on, they replied that someone had crept up on the Americans and pinched their sten guns, and it was assumed that whoever it was, were off down the road towards the Japanese camp to have a go at killing some of them. Who could blame them? However, the yanks must have caught up with them, and persuaded them to return to camp, because a short while later the jeep returned and four of our lads got out. The following morning they were reprimanded by the RSM. We did however, find out later that in some camps, guards and Japs had been killed by prisoners, in fact it was heard that in one case a gunso had been slaughtered with his own sword.

The next few days past peacefully, patiently waiting for someone to get us out, we got news daily from India via the yanks radio. Thankfully the worry of my ulcer began to recede, the medical orderlies had ground some white tablets to powder, we called them M&B. the powder applied daily seemed to be working as it was not so angry looking, but still extremely painful to clean. The next few days past uneventfully and on the 24th of August the two yanks told us that they were moving out the next day 25th and if we would like to write a few lines to send home they would see that they got to the UK. We only had pieces of toilet paper that had been dropped from the planes. We wrote a message on one side folded them twice and wrote our home address. When I eventually arrived home, my parents told me that they had received the note in a few days.

Readers may be interested to see a scanned copy of the original.

(On the following page is a scanned copy of the first letter sent upon release, written on toilet paper.)

On the morning of 8th September 1945 we were told to dress in full KD, (Khaki Drill) as we were going to have a visitor to talk to us. Early afternoon we were ordered on parade and a short while later a Land Rover arrived, out stepped several British officers and a female. Standing in front of us she began to speak. "I am Lady Mount Batten, I have come to see for myself the conditions in which you have been living. I sincerely hope that we can get you all home as soon as possible. You will be leaving this camp today to fly to Rangoon, to be prepared for your journey home by sea. I hope you have a very happy and pleasant journey. The Japanese have had their instructions, they have been ordered to take you by road from this camp and all the way to the plane, you will not even have to walk across the tarmac." We were then fallen out and she toured the camp and talked to individual POWs. On the way back to her vehicle we all waved and cheered, as she was about to get in, she turned and shouted, "You can now get back into your jap happies if you wish."

Sure enough that evening at about six o'clock army vehicles each driven by a single Japanese rolled into camp. They did not get out and we did not speak or have anything to do with them, we piled in, and the convoy set off. It was a very uncomfortable and bumpy journey, but the heat of the day had subsided, we could not care less, we were on our way. The journey took all night and we eventually arrived at Bangkok airport, and taken to a large empty hangar, where food had been prepared, after which we were divided into groups of twenty five men, to wait for our plane. A shuttle service of a number of Lockheeds had been arranged for the journey to

Dear Mother and Father,

Overjoyed and happy looking Dad. The date is 25 August 1945. At present we are still in POW camps in (THAILAND) waiting for ships to take us away. The Americans are moving off first, and we are sending these notes with them, in the hope that they will post them and on to you at the first opportunity.

I have received about 10 letters from you during POW life but have only been able to fill in Post cards twice a year. Some of those you have not received, as we know they have never left camp. I am quite fit and am looking forward to getting home to you for Christmas. Cannot send you any address to write to, but I will send telegram letter every available opportunity.

I will send you more news when I get to civilisation with more paper. Love to all.

Your loving Son

Roy

Rangoon. When my groups turn came some hours later a truck driven by a Japanese drove us to the side of the plane, we alighted, climbed into the plane and immediately took off. We seated ourselves each side of the plane facing inwards. The pilot and co-pilot put the plane on automatic pilot and came out of their cockpit and sat on the floor between us to talk and ask questions about our life as prisoners. Suddenly, the plane began to fall like a stone, my stomach seemed to hit the roof of the cabin and our faces all turned green, we had run into an air pocket. The pilot jumped up and made a dive for the cockpit, passing through the door he got a nasty cut on his arm. I looked through the window and saw we had dropped to just a few feet above the sea, what a fright. Luckily we regained height, in doing so we entered some stormy weather, the pilot said he would climb and fly above it. We eventually landed in Rangoon without any further problems. I found out later that during the several days that this operation took place, one or two planes had in fact not been so lucky and had dropped into the sea, drowning all on board. How unlucky can you get, after surviving three and a half years in the hell camps.

Alighting from the plane, a short journey by bus brought us to quiet pleasant suburb and a large building. Girls from the WRVS. (Women's Royal Voluntary Services) stood waiting outside and showed us into a large room with tables decked with table clothes, flowers, fruit and cigarettes. We sat down and enjoyed being waited on by the girls. It was a very memorable and joyful reception. Apparently the building was being used to provide a hospital service, not knowing our state of health. Being reasonable under the circumstances, except for a bandage over my ulcer, I was directed outside into a large tent, the floor was completely covered with coconut matting, along each side stood a row of single beds already made and covered with white sheets and best of all a lovely white pillow. During the next few days we just enjoyed the luxury of being free, relaxing on our lovely beds, reading several daily newspapers flown in from the UK. The papers were of great interest as, not only to read the latest news, they also gave an indication of the many changes that had taken place, during our years of captivity. We also enjoyed being waited on by the WRVS at meal times. The food to our surprise consisted of a normal diet but in reduced quantities. After what we had been used to, we found it to be very rich. The hospital was then treating my ulcer twice daily and it was noticeably showing signs of healing completely. One morning we all lay resting on our beds, enjoying our freedom when a uniformed officer walked into our tent. We instantly recognised him, it was Lord Louis Mount Batten, he smiled came towards my bed and sat down on it. He signalled to all the others in the tent and said, "Would you all gather round I want to have a chat." He spent quite a while with us in an effort to boost our moral by telling us about the campaign in Burma and best of all, the many thousands of Japanese that had been killed by our troops. We spent about ten days in the hospital, I have no record of the actual day we left Rangoon, but I do remember standing at the rail of the ship, the 'SS Orduna' and looking back at the receding shoreline. Many thoughts passed through my mind, beginning with a feeling of overwhelming sadness. Leaving behind in the region of 20,000 comrades, who had died and been buried in unknown graves, mostly in that dreadful jungle alongside what we then called, 'The Railway of Death.' What a waste of young lives. My thoughts went way back to those first weeks after being taken prisoner, when those running sores on my face prevented me from going on the first working party to leave Changi with my mate Douglas, the lad I had left England with, because of his broken engagement. I was never to see him again. I eventually heard that he had died of dysentery and starvation in one of those dreadful jungle camps in December 1942. I also realised that I would have to face his parents, on my return to the UK. A recent letter from home told me that the two families, having something in common, had become friendly.

Unlike previous journeys by sea, this time we had adequate living space around our bunks. It was very refreshing spending time on deck, after the steamy heat of Thailand and Burma. On the 25th of September 1945 the 'Orduna' dropped anchor just off Colombo, Ceylon, (as it was called then). We were taken ashore in boats, on the dock side an Indian Regimental Band played the victory march and women from the WRNS (Women's Royal Naval Services) took us in buses to a large building in a park. We then with more girls enjoyed a meal on tables decked with flowers, cigarettes and beer, it was a wonderful reception. We spent three hours ashore and at 4pm were taken back to the ship which set sail again the following morning 26th September1945.

Our next port of call turned out to be Port Said. We docked on the Sunday 7th October 1945. went ashore to be issued with a full kit. We would soon be needing it as we reached the cooler climate. After passing through the Suez Canal we entered the Med and immediately felt a change in the climate to the extent that, for the first time in nearly five years began to feel cold. We changed clothes, discarding and packing our tropical kit.

We spent more time below decks, it was quite boring, thank goodness there was a library and cinema aboard to help pass away the time. Soon we were passing through the Bay of Biscay. It was a miserable passage, the ship although quite big rolled and tossed. The rolling gave me a sick stomach but I was not sick, I was not as bad as some of the other lads. One morning mackerel was on the menu for breakfast, I love them and the only way I could eat my fish was by lying down full length on my back on a form. I managed it without being sick.

Eventually we spotted the coastline of England, and again a lump rose in my throat, what a relief we all felt. Sailing up the coast we entered the Mersey to dock at Liverpool on the 22nd of October 1945. Someone must have given notice of our impending arrival, all the boats and ships on our approach immediately started to sound their sirens, their crews stood at their rails shouting and waiving. What a reception we got, as the ship docked, hundreds of people stood on the dock side clapping, and shouting good luck, and waiving like mad. We had already packed when the order was given to disembark. Struggling through the crowd on the dock side and into buses, which quickly conveyed us to a military building in the city, where Medical Officers waited to give each man a medical. As I was reasonably OK I had no problem. I was declared fit for immediate leave pending discharge. Even though we had been on a very good diet since release, two months previous and had put on a little weight. When they weighed me, I just about tipped the scales at seven stone. Within two hours we had been issued with, army pay book, ration book, clothing coupons, advance of pay and a railway warrant from Liverpool Lime Street Station to my home town. It was all over. I was on my way home.

The Queen and I bid you a very warm welcome home.
Through all the great trials and sufferings which
you have undergone at the hands of the Japanese, you
and your comrades have been constantly in our thoughts.
We know from the accounts we have already received how
heavy those sufferings have been. We know also that
these have been endured by you with the highest courage.

We mourn with you the deaths of so many of your
gallant comrades.

With all our hearts, we hope that your return from
captivity will bring you and your families a full measure
of happiness, which you may long enjoy together.

George R.I.

September 1945.

Copy of a letter from King George VI - September 1945

A message from all those mates left behind:

When you go home tell them of me,
for their tomorrow, I gave my today.

There was no shame when grown men cried,
as they scattered poppies on those who died.

Of hunger, disease and arduous toil,
they now lay in peace on foreign soil.

These were our mates we knew so well,
like us they suffered a living hell.

Abide with me, with feeling we sing,
not forgetting but remembering.

Those immortal words, nor years condemn,
we who returned will remember them.

Written and reproduced by courtesy of Len Sheppard, FEPOW

The Forgotten Army

Chungkai POW cemetery, (recent picture.)

Copies of this book are available through
Horseshoe Publications and can be
obtained from good book shops or bought
directly from the publisher via the internet
at - www.InfinityJunction.com

Published by Infinity Junction.
Infinity Junction works in association with
Horseshoe Publications and inter-read